URBAN PLANNING ASPECTS OF
WATER POLLUTION CONTROL

INSTITUTE OF URBAN ENVIRONMENT
COLUMBIA UNIVERSITY

SIGURD GRAVA

URBAN PLANNING
ASPECTS OF WATER
POLLUTION CONTROL

COLUMBIA UNIVERSITY PRESS   1969

NEW YORK AND LONDON

Sigurd Grava is Associate Professor of Urban Planning
at Columbia University

Copyright © 1969 Columbia University Press
Library of Congress Catalog Card Number: 72-87147
Printed in the United States of America

FOREWORD

This book is one of the first of a series of works dealing with urban affairs to be published by the Institute of Urban Environment, Columbia University. Several others are presently in preparation, including a model of process for physical planning, a study of citizen participation in city rebuilding, an exploration of developmental problems in semi-arid regions, and a survey of regional planning in Turkey. As these subject areas indicate, the Institute is involved in a program of research that is international in scope and wide-ranging in interest. The Institute's objective since its founding in 1966 has been to illuminate the key problems of urban areas through research investigations designed both to gauge the magnitude of need and evaluate the recommended positive policies for meeting that need.

Urban Planning Aspects of Water Pollution Control is a study that examines one dimension of the total physical planning dilemma facing cities throughout the world. The major thrust of Dr. Grava's study has been to analyze the problem of waste disposal as it imposes a constraint on the policy choices available to the urban planner. Thus, the basic engineering difficulties involved are treated as an adjunct to planning issues. In discussing water pollution control measures, Dr. Grava moves from detailed technical information and its planning implications to the question of its effects on community organization. Particular attention is given to the special problems of disposal in developing countries.

Historically, the ability to dispose of waste was a strong determinant of tolerable population densities in urban settlements and indeed often of survival itself. With our improved ability to understand and control wastes that has come with modern technology, the spectrum of possibilities available to us in urban development has broadened greatly. High population densities in compact urban areas have shed their once onerous health problems and now can become viable, productive communities. This change is of special importance in developing countries, where the construction of efficient industrial cities is often the primary component of national development plans.

It is our hope that this study by Dr. Grava will prove one of the seminal works in this new and potentially valuable aspect of the urban planning process. In future years the coordination he recommends between the traditional components of physical planning and pollution control factors will be, I am sure, a working part of a general planning practice.

New York, April 1969 *Chester Rapkin*
DIRECTOR, INSTITUTE OF
URBAN ENVIRONMENT

ACKNOWLEDGMENTS

All the work involved in the preparation of this book has been sponsored by the Institute of Urban Environment, Columbia University. The funds, in turn, came from a grant of the Ford Foundation.

Thus this publication is entirely the result of the Institute's concern with urban problems, including the one discussed here. Major credit for the initiation and completion of this study is due Dr. Chester Rapkin, Director of the Institute, for his active interest and general guidance. The encouragement and support received from Mr. Charles Abrams, the former Chairman of the Division of Urban Planning at Columbia University, was most helpful.

Many of my friends and colleagues have read the manuscript and have offered suggestions and constructive criticisms. In particular, I wish to acknowledge the contributions of Dr. Grace Milgram, Mr. Francis Ferguson, Dr. Otto H. Koenigsberger, Mr. Joseph K. Murphy, and Dr. Granville H. Sewell. They can take credit for many improvements in the work, but, as is always the case, they are not responsible for any of its shortcomings.

The research work was aided materially by Walter Collins, a graduate student at Columbia University. The illustrations were prepared by Thomas J. Thomas, who was a teaching assistant and Ph.D. candidate.

New York, April 1969   *Sigurd Grava*

CONTENTS

ABBREVIATIONS

APHA	American Public Health Association
ASCE	American Society of Civil Engineers
NAS	National Academy of Sciences
USPHS	United States Public Health Service
WHO	World Health Organization
WPCF	Water Pollution Control Federation

INTRODUCTION

During the last few years, urban and regional planners have discovered that in addition to the numerous aspects presently accepted as standard considerations in the preparation of plans, studies, and policy statements for cities and regions another element has to be included: environmental pollution control or, as it is sometimes called, waste management.

This is not, of course, a new urban problem, yet it has emerged just recently as a basic and vital concern not only in the public health area, but also in the structuring and organization of communities. It enters, thus, within the province of the planner.

ATTITUDE TOWARD WASTE CONTROL

Pollution and waste accumulation have plagued us ever since man started living in permanent settlements, and a multitude of solutions have been developed throughout the centuries reflecting contemporary attitudes toward sanitation and ideas with respect to a decent environment. Man has always been careful to remove wastes from his own private dwelling, but he usually has dumped them immediately outside. This inherent public irresponsibility is a curious, albeit apparently basic, human characteristic which was in evidence in the ancient advanced civilizations and is still with us today. The organized community must therefore protect itself against the negligence of its own members through regulations, public works programs, and enforcement of quality levels as defined by itself.

Medieval society tended to ignore the problem almost entirely, often with dire consequences. Some American Indian tribes simply moved their camp when the conditions became intolerable even according to their standards. During the early Industrial Revolution city fathers paid some lip service to the need for waste control, but did little since their interests were centered elsewhere.

The medical profession was the first to discover the real effects of pollution on human health and well-being during the last century or so, a period that has been characterized by rapid advances in medical science. Sanitary engineers and public health experts have done much in more recent decades in the development of methods and techniques toward waste control. The time has come to apply this knowledge not as the basis for stop-gap and emergency measures in crisis situations but in a systematic and preventative way for all urban settlements, regions, and, indeed, the environment as a whole. If information or experience is still lacking in certain areas, it must be identified and the gap filled through research and experimentation. A positive and constructive approach is required through (1) the definition of problems; (2) decisions as to what should be done or what levels of quality to be achieved; (3) the development of the appropriate technological methods; and, (4) the application of such solutions within a given or modified political and administrative framework.

CURRENT TRENDS

In a democratic society, such work must be supported or at least understood by the public at large. Many professionals, including planners, have tried for some time to show that the pollution problem is becoming more crucial with every year, but these voices were met with widespread apathy. Habits and attitudes developed over centuries are not easily changed. It appears, however, that the message has finally penetrated, aided primarily by the facts that environmental conditions in a number of our huge metropolitan areas have truly reached crisis proportions—back to medieval levels—and that the popular press has joined the battle.

The mid-1960s may be remembered as the turning point and the nadir in urban pollution control. Today there is a general public awareness of the problem and a strong willingness to do something about it. Equally important, we have also recognized that work with the symptoms (partial treatment of the final effluents) cannot hope to achieve meaningful results; we must get at the root of the problem which may involve control of the use of certain materials and production processes, will require regional cooperation, and should include careful spatial distribution of activities.

SCOPE AND ORIENTATION OF STUDY

Much of this is the task of a planner, yet it is a new field for him, and he may not be familiar with the technical information, or even have a method of approach and procedure defined that would introduce pollution considerations into the routine planning work.

The purpose of this monograph is to serve as an aid to the planner by offering a discussion of the various techniques and methods currently available in water pollution control and their role in community organization. The investigation is based primarily upon the experience in the industrially advanced countries, but the problems encountered in developing countries are considered also. The aim is not to prepare a precise how-to-do-it handbook but rather to present a survey and evaluation of current practices (state of art) and discuss future needs and possibilities as related to community building and planning.

The discussion is limited strictly to water-borne wastes and water quality control. This is not because atmospheric pollution and solid waste disposal are not equally important, but simply in order to keep the discussion focused and manageable. It is hoped that, outside of the purely technical considerations, the basic approach established in the control of one type of waste may also be valid for others, and it must be stressed that, since all three types of wastes can be transformed from one state in any of the two others and often are thus changed during the handling process, all three of them must be considered together in the effort to establish a meaningful and efficient waste control program for any region or locality.

The basic outline of this monograph is the following:
Chapter 1 is devoted to a general discussion of the liquid waste problem and establishes a framework for analysis and control measures;

Chapter 2 considers the economic and functional characteristics of water systems which demand a comprehensive and regionwide approach;

Chapters 3, 4, 5, and 6 contain material of a rather specific nature which provides the background information needed in planning for waste control (sources of pollutants, treatment systems, administrative and financial considerations);

Chapter 7 discusses the implications of liquid waste control in planning terms and as a component of community organization. As such, this chapter represents the major focus of the work;

Chapter 8 investigates the particular modifications that are necessary in water pollution control in developing countries.

A glossary of the various terms, which appear in the text but are not always defined therein, is provided for easy reference at the end of the work. Several appendices contain precise technical data which may be of use to the planner. A selected annotated bibliography lists sources for further information in the field.

This work is to be regarded, however, as an early approach to a practically new subdiscipline, and, consequently, it is certain that many additions and modifications will emerge in the near future. Therefore, each chapter concludes with a listing of needed research, recognizing gaps in knowledge that exist at the present.

1

FEATURES OF THE PROBLEM

A few years from now, a group of astronauts, or cosmonauts, will be traveling in a space capsule toward a distant planet. They will be living in a closed ecological environment: breathing air which will be recirculated, drinking purified and reconstituted liquid wastes, and burning solid wastes for auxiliary power. Nothing will be dumped out in space; on longer trips this matter may even be used as organic raw material for food growing.[1]

Meanwhile, back on spaceship Earth, also a closed ecological system, less than a billion of us living in the so-called technologically advanced communities will utilize disposal systems for our bodily wastes which often succeed in removing the unmentionable stuff from sight, but which also allow most of the original components to return to haunt us in a modified form in our air, soil, and water.

More than 2 billion residents of villages and cities in the developing regions and of rural areas across the world will depend on a hole in the ground, often overflowing, as man has done for many millennia.

The problem basically is that there are so many of us living so close together in urban clusters that the great capacity of the natural environment to purify itself is submerged by the flood of filth we

---

[1] See W. O. Pipes, *Waste-Recovery Processes for a Closed Ecological System* (reference 93 in Annotated Bibliography) and L. G. Rich, et al., *Waste Disposal on Space Craft and Its Bearing on Terrestrial Problems* (reference 96).

generate. And we lack, or are not willing to spend, resources to help nature along.

AREAS OF CONCERN

We all know that there is a serious water pollution problem. For a few years now the press has picked up the cry, and it makes good copy: Hudson River, Calumet Harbor in Chicago, Potomac River, and Lake Erie have become household words that in no way lessens the disgrace that they represent. Nor are these conditions unique to the United States. In Europe the struggle has lasted for a longer time and reached more critical dimensions because of higher average development densities. Yet, there has also been a number of encouraging events in Europe as a positive response to an urgent need: the Ruhr water resources management system in Germany can serve as a model for others; fish have been observed recently in the Thames indicating a reversal in pollution levels; and research and development continues there of treatment facilities, particularly those promising a higher degree of purity.

Investigations[2] have shown that one half of United States communities with over 2,500 population do not have adequate sewage disposal facilities. About 65 billion gallons of raw sewage is discharged untreated in streams and lakes each year. New York City alone dumps 400,000 gallons each day in its rivers; Detroit, the fourth largest city in the country, has only a crude and superficial screening process.

The most serious problems in environmental pollution at the present time can be found in almost all the developing countries, particularly in their cities which are receiving staggering amounts of inmigrants but are not able to provide all the required public services, notably sewers and other sanitary utilities. While there is some hope that the cities in the industrialized countries are on the way toward improvements—at least they have the technical knowledge, an inventory of existing improvements, public demand for action, and

[2] U.S. Congress, House Subcommittee on Science, Research and Development, November 1966.

POPULATION SERVICED BY SEWERS
IN THE UNITED STATES

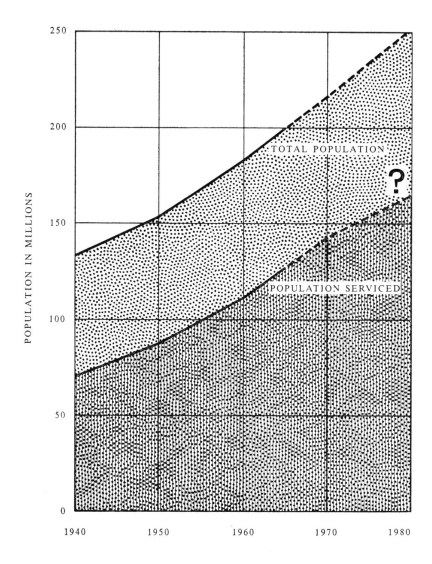

reasonable investment resources—the situation in the developing countries is deteriorating.

Nor is the problem limited to urban environments. The unfortunate experiences of the past in the reckless and wanton exploitation of natural resources that has destroyed or seriously damaged scenic and recreational areas, fishlife, soils, and other economic and visual assets, are repeatedly forgotten, and new examples emerge continuously in regions which were until now untouched by the predatory actions of man. Thus, leaching acid from mines in Appalachia is today killing the rivers of that area. Pulp mills in Sweden have polluted inland water to such an extent that fish caught in forty lakes and rivers have been declared unfit for human consumption because of high methyl mercury contents.[3] Lake Baikal in the USSR, which holds one fifth of the world's lake water and contains a unique biota, stands in danger of irreversible pollution by wastes from a new giant pulp mill.[4]

In effect, while everybody as an individual is concerned about the environment, there is no one responsible directly and specifically for its quality. Any number of public agencies enter into the field, but their actions are rarely coordinated; and the waste disposal practices of private business and establishments are not fully controlled.

Our great and rapid strides in technology have enabled us to develop a series of new and useful products; our efficient marketing systems can distribute these widely and almost instantaneously. Yet this has also eliminated the practical testing over a period of time of the secondary or unforeseen effects of such products on the environment. A number of different fertilizers, pesticides, detergents, and non-reductible containers are all recent offenses against natural conditions and quality.

But there are also some bright spots. The technology of waste neutralization and treatment is being improved, and greater effectiveness and lower unit costs can be anticipated. Federal government, as well as the public, has agreed to participate in and encourage pollution control through emerging appropriate legislation and financial aid. Industrialists are exercising greater care in the disposal of their wastes—voluntarily or under community pressure. Suitable

---

[3] *Science News,* December 1967.
[4] *The New York Times,* July 2, 1967

large-scale regional control agencies are becoming effective in some locations.

SUGGESTED APPROACH

The main and most urgent arenas for action still remain the cities or, more precisely, the urbanized regions, most of which unquestionably will continue to grow. But it is not only a question of providing services for the additional increments of population—there is an urgent demand for the revamping and improvement of existing facilities to bring them up to current standards which, incidentally, are constantly moving upward. There is an even greater need to rethink and reorganize our approach to pollution control. Instead of piecemeal palliatives and localized stop-gap measures, a systematic and coordinated attack is required on a continuous basis. That is, a permanent management organization in each region which controls the location of activities and their effluent discharges, has the means to enforce standards and/or operate treatment facilities, and monitors the performance of the entire system.

Such a physical and administrative structure is indicated graphically in Fig. 2 and can be regarded as the framework for the following discussion and description of the various elements and considerations. While these relationships are intended to illustrate liquid waste problems, they could also be applied easily to other types of wastes.

WASTE GENERATION AND DUMPING

Each activity, whether it is that of a family residence or a steel mill, produces wastes or unusable by-products which represent a liability since they have no practical utility for the generating establishment. Traditionally, these wastes have been discharged or dumped on the ground, into water, or into atmosphere without or with only some limited treatment, i.e., the removal of the more offensive components of the wastes, and their reduction to less harmful forms. The effluents are thus regarded as completely negative materials.

The other approach to waste handling is recycling: an attempt to

THE WASTE CYCLE

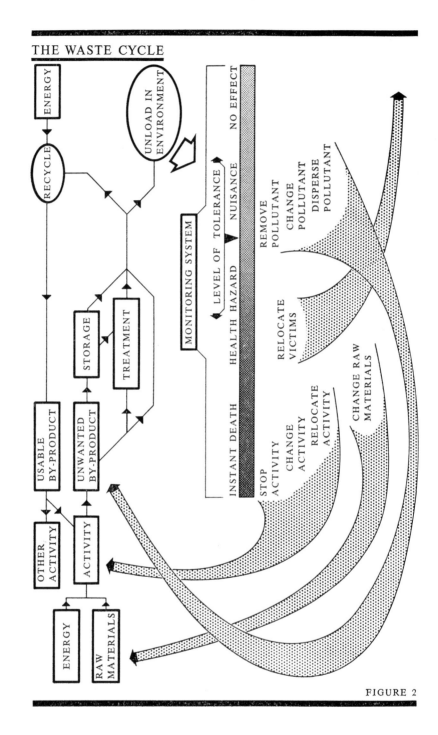

FIGURE 2

reconstitute many components of the discharges into usable materials, and to recirculate them back to the same or other productive or consumer activities. Water itself is not the least of such salvable materials. In the past, reuse was only considered if the resultant end products themselves paid for the necessary energy and labor input in the recycling process. Today, such direct economic justification has to be broadened to include also such less tangible aspects as the gradual exhaustion of disposal sites, public demand for a clean environment, and recognition of a wide range of social costs generally. In a long-term perspective, recycling appears as the only logical and feasible approach to the problem, since all other methods place cumulative loads on the environment.

However, at the present time, disposal methods that rely largely on the capacity of the environment to absorb and dilute pollutants are still often utilized and will continue to be utilized. If pollutants are discharged in small enough quantities, they are gradually reduced to inoffensive materials through natural processes and reenter the biological food or water cycles. Yet, in urban areas the amounts discharged are almost invariably far in excess of the natural absorptive capacities of soil, air, or water. Consequently, the natural ecological balance is upset, and recreational and functional resources are destroyed.

The impact of pollution may range over a wide scale: from a slight discomfort for some very sensitive species of trout to instantaneous death of all biological life forms. Since perfect purity of the environment is not possible nor necessary, a "level of tolerance" has to be established for various areas depending on local circumstances. In the past this threshold was not defined precisely but rather arrived at by an implied consensus in response to the then prevailing attitude toward pollution—a vague point at which the community started to worry or felt that something has to be done.

Today, again, such an approach is not satisfactory since, in order to apply scientific methods with the greatest possible efficiency, accurately defined objectives in precise terms are required. As will be shown later, the basic task of setting standards is by no means an easy one.

TREATMENT METHODS

Depending on the amount by which pollution exceeds permissible levels, a number of corrective actions can be instituted which usually demand an active participation or control by public agencies, since there is no economic incentive for the polluter to do it voluntarily. Treatment of wastes usually costs far in excess of what the returns would be to the individual producing them. The fact that such action would result in great benefit to the entire community is not of significant importance to the producer; therefore, the community must protect itself, through enforcement and direct action, against abuses by the individuals.

However, before starting the list of potential remedial methods, it should be noted that in the waste management field, too, prevention as a basic concept is eminently applicable. In an overall analysis, it can be often shown that the inconvenience and costs associated with *not* producing waste in the first place can be considerably less than trying to neutralize it later after it has been introduced in the environment. The problem here is again one of private vs. public costs, respectively, and the establishment of a regulatory mechanism whereby the individual waste producer is forced to assume responsibility (financial and other) for his own wastes.

However, since the reduction of waste generation even in the best of circumstances cannot be complete, other procedures must be employed; the basic types are listed below in a sequence approximating their severity.

First, the pollutant may be dispersed, i.e., sprinkled over the environment, thus preventing concentrations in excess of the local natural absorptive capacity. Examples of this may be the discharge of small volumes of sewage through numerous well-spaced outlets into a large river, or the construction of individual septic tanks for residences in a suburban area. Thus, instead of having heavy pollution at few locations, all the area is slightly but tolerably affected. This practice, if kept within limits, would be acceptable. However, because in most instances large quantities of waste are generated and discharged at very specific and limited locations, such solutions are rarely feasible or reliable over a period of time.

The next step is to change the state of the pollutant through the reduction of the offensive elements to a less harmful form or to one with which the environment can cope more successfully even though large effluent volumes may be involved. Most of the standard sewage treatment processes do exactly that and no more: they oxidize the organic material, or allow it to be digested by micro-organisms, producing an inert material which does not react biochemically farther.

The same treatment processes also often accomplish the next task which is the removal of most of the pollutants in the form of sludge. Yet, this action by itself is not adequate since the concentrated material cannot be accumulated indefinitely but must be processed further through the use of the previous two approaches: reduction (sludge digestion, for example) or dispersal (use as agricultural fertilizer, for example).

This is the limit of routine sanitary engineering work: handling of the wastes themselves as they are generated. It must be noted that the processes, popularly regarded as the solution, can be quite thorough and efficient. But most such public works improvements do not remove all the pollutants, they can generate noisome by-products, and they cannot achieve maximum efficiency in waste control since they deal only with the effects, not causes.

WORK WITH THE CAUSES OF POLLUTION

The next group of actions involve an attack of the problem at a more basic level, going directly to the producers of pollution. The exercise of governmental responsibility, hopefully based on equitable standards and planning thought, is required at this level. There have been numerous instances throughout urban history where completely intolerable abuses of the environment, produced by such places as slaughter houses and tanneries, have had to be stopped by fiat. This, however, also means that the community has been negligent in allowing a polluter to start and continue operations to reach a situation where only a drastic corrective action is possible.

It is suggested instead that these decisions be made prior to the construction of facilities and commencement of operations to preclude pollution or even to reduce the anticipated loads on treatment facilities.

In other words, planning is needed which is based on a full understanding as to what discharges are to be expected or are to be permitted at any given location, and what their effect will be on the environment. If these loads cannot be reasonably accommodated by the future waste collection and treatment facilities, which themselves are subject to design decisions allowing a range of capacities, a number of avenues are open.

The most drastic of these would be simply to bar the polluting activity from a given site, or, if it has an undeniable reason for locating at a particular position and has great economic or social significance, then the area has to be proscribed for all those activities which would be adversely affected by the primary establishment. In this last case, a careful analysis would be required to determine whether full treatment of the obnoxious discharges is not a better and cheaper solution than a complete disruption in the land use development of a large sector. The answer for any particular case can only be given within the context of an entire regional plan under a comprehensive study program.

Finally, the pollution problem can often be eliminated or at least reduced by modifications or adjustments in the activity itself (or in the production process under question) or through the switch to raw materials which are prone to produce less external pollution, as suggested previously. This is a solution, however, which cannot be subjected to public control directly; it must be accomplished through the establishment of performance or effluent standards (type and maximum amount of emissions permitted) and allowing the private firm or individual to decide whether to change the process, use other materials, build extensive effluent treatment facilities, or move out entirely.

An ever present consideration with any one of the approaches outlined above is the question of costs, since none of them can be accomplished without some, often great, expenditures directly or indirectly. The problem is primarily to determine how the costs should be apportioned between the public bodies, the pollution generators, and those affected by the discharges. We will return to this aspect several times in the following pages.

It is also rather obvious that to achieve satisfactory pollution control in any given locality, any combination of the above approaches may have to be employed. They represent together the inventory of basic actions that can be effectuated through the use of various detailed methods. The rest of this monograph is largely devoted to a discussion of these latter aspects.

2

WATERSHED SYSTEMS: REGIONAL ASPECTS

To support the argument that water pollution problems have to be examined and handled within the context of an entire watershed basin, only one fact has to be stated: the flow of water in rivers and creeks has no respect for political boundaries but it follows a constant pattern from surface run-off to progressively larger waterways, always in the same direction and with cumulative volumes. This is becoming increasingly recognized not only as an abstract and theoretical concept but also as a guiding principle in those action programs that succeed in breaking through the restraints imposed by tradition, inertia, or inadequate understanding. For example, the Advisory Commission on Intergovernmental Relations has prepared an approximate ranking of fifteen governmental functions as to whether they can be best performed at local or areawide level. Starting with fire protection and public education as the "most local," the list concludes with planning, water supply and sewage disposal, and air pollution control as the activities where maximum efficiency can only be expected if they are attacked on a regional scale.

To support the argument that water pollution problems have to be examined and handled within a systems[1] framework, again only

---

[1] The purpose of this work is not to examine in detail the various elements which would enter into a precise systems analysis of the pollution problem nor to construct a model which could be used for reliable calculations. At the

one fact is significant: water of any given source may be used for a multitude of purposes ranging from human consumption to the production of power. And this use may be sequential. Since commonly the requirements, including the necessary degree of purity, are different for each of the various types of users, their demands have to be weighed against each other to define a management program which can satisfy multiple objectives and criteria and to achieve this with the least total cost to society.

Water is a scarce resource not so much in terms of quantity as of quality at any given point in space for a particular purpose. Almost all social or productive uses of water introduce pollutants into it, and the claims for the best quality water have to be balanced among various functional interests, local political jurisdictions, and even regions. The allocation and control of this desirable material thus becomes not only a governmental responsibility, but one which must be exercised in a rational manner that often attempts to achieve only compromise solutions.

CURRENT WORK IN SYSTEMS ANALYSIS

ECONOMIC MODELS. The work up to now in river basin studies, employing the new method of systems approach, has concentrated on the economic aspects of water management[2] correlating the needs for irrigation and power production to fluctuating river levels or flow volumes. Without detracting in any way from the importance and validity of such studies, these investigations concern themselves with only a few of the functions which a water channel has to perform, i.e., those which can be expressed most readily in dollar amounts in a cost-benefit structure.

The use of water as raw material in domestic and industrial processes is dependent on its quality, or rather its degree of pollution

---

present stage of our knowledge and methodology, this is not yet quite possible, although a number of pioneering efforts are under way. The attempt here will be to describe in rather qualitative terms what the components of such a system should be and how they relate to each other.

[2] The most advanced study of this kind is the one prepared by Harvard University and published as *Design of Water-Resource Systems* by A. A. Maas, et al. (reference 81).

which is the reverse concept. Various levels of purity of available water represent corresponding, albeit difficult to define and quantify, benefits to the several users. In a strict systems framework these benefits have to be expressed as direct savings in terms of dollars in the preparation or handling costs of water for the various users, including even such seemingly peripheral considerations as the cost of buying drinking water for family consumption if the municipal supply has noticeable taste or odor. Furthermore, these determinations should most likely be weighted or modified according to the importance of each particular user to the society as a whole. On top of everything else, very high levels of pollution will not be acceptable to the community from an esthetic and psychological point of view even if this would appear to be the most economical solution. That is, the public may be willing to bear a considerable amount of expenditures for pollution control to satisfy its demand for a decent environment even if it has no tangible monetary return. But, since commercial users would also benefit from such investment, should they contribute to the overall costs to reach these levels, or should they only be responsible for the incremental expenses created because of their demand for even cleaner waters? [3] And, going back, we may ask, should the community force the original polluters to clean their effluent to such an extent that esthetic sensibilities are not offended, or should the public itself pay for its newly discovered demands?

Finally, there are the underlying problems of most economic models: uncertainty in the identification of all the pertinent variables, and lack of knowledge as to what the total long-range costs to the society will be if positive action is not taken.

MONITORING MODELS. The other area of emphasis in current work has been the development of predictive models which would have the capability to estimate pollution levels at points along the river in response to various effluent loadings and river flow conditions. [4]

[3] Valuable insights in this and related aspects can be found in several of the essays included in *Environmental Quality in a Growing Economy* edited by H. Jarrett (reference 64).

[4] See, for example, D. P. Loucks, *Wastewater Treatment Systems Analysis* (reference 79).

These determinations, usually based on a calculation of dissolved oxygen levels as a measure of pollution, can be used to regulate discharges in order to assure acceptable conditions at all times. This work can be bolstered in actual practice by the establishment of monitoring stations to serve as checking devices in a continuous surveillance of water quality.[5]

It can be suggested, however, that in the future a marriage will have to be achieved that combines the concepts of the economic evaluation of resource management and the maintenance of acceptable environmental quality through surveillance methods. There can be little question that such a comprehensive planning and operational system would be a logical approach not only toward solving the pollution problem but also for the establishment of a rational and efficient basis for the management of a critical resource.

At the same time, it must be admitted that there are still a number of obstacles in the way before the contemplated organizations, as described herein, can be put into effect.

For example, there is a need for additional technical information, especially relating different sewage discharges to water quality levels; public acceptance and cooperation between various political bodies has to be achieved in a number of instances. The experience of some of the agencies of this type presently operating gives promise that the latter aspect can be solved.

WATERSHED MANAGEMENT ORGANIZATIONS

All the above are still theoretical studies; it is perhaps even more important to note that there are several examples, within the United States and elsewhere, where the necessity of river basin planning and control has been recognized and is being exercised through traditional and conventional methods. In a number of places this has taken an economic orientation, such as the TVA and organizations for certain rivers in the western United States (such as Colorado, Rio Grande, Columbia, Sacramento, and San Joaquin) which have been in

---

[5] A concise discussion of wastewater analyses is given on pages S-8 to S-11 of *"Waste Water Treatment,"* a special report in *Power* magazine, June 1967 (reference 82).

operation for a number of years. Numerous flood-control commissions with extensive interests exist also. In the last decade or so, other ventures have been started which are more pollution-oriented or have included a greater variety of purposes within their areas of concern. The Delaware,[6] Ohio,[7] the Southeast Basins,[8] and others are examples currently in operation. In a number of other watersheds, steps are being taken to set up similar joint multipurpose management programs: Hudson, Potomac, and others.

The experience and accomplishments of the water pollution control program for the Ruhr district in Germany have been cited often and described in many publications.[9] One of the few truly remarkable success stories in this otherwise bleak area, it warrants a brief discussion here too, particularly because the control programs were started well after water pollution had become a serious problem.

The Ruhrverband is a cooperative association of management authorities which has been given extensive operational and enforcement powers by higher levels of government. Since the organization of this system in 1904(!), the Ruhrverband has been able to restore water recreational use within one of the heaviest industrial areas of the world served by rivers with relatively low flow levels.

The engineering works are interesting and impressive, but the more significant features are found in the administrative and management structure. Briefly, it is based on an allocation of the expenses involved in running the system according to the discharge loads of individual polluters—industries or municipalities. That is, there is an effluent charge which reflects the theoretical waste treatment costs for each and is based, for industries, on the level of production,

[6] Delaware River Basin Commission.

[7] Ohio River Valley Sanitation Commission (ORSANCO) since 1948. See E. J. Cleary, *The ORSANCO Story: Water Quality Management in the Ohio Valley under an Interstate Compact* (Baltimore: The Johns Hopkins Press, 1967), 335 pp.

[8] See C. E. Kindsvater (ed.), *Organization and Methodology for River Basin Planning* (reference 70).

[9] See D. R. Maneval, "Western European Wastewater Treatment—Part 2," *Water and Sewage Works,* July 1967, pp. 239–42; A. V. Kneese, "Water Quality Management by Regional Authorities in the Ruhr Area," pp. 109–29, in *Controlling Pollution* (reference 43); A. V. Kneese, "The Ruhr and the Delaware," pp. 83–92, in *Journal of the Sanitary Engineering Division,* ASCE, October 1966.

number of employees, waste flow volume, and character according to
a rather complex formula. These charges provide the funds to operate
the treatment works, sewage channels, pumping stations, and storage
reservoirs as a completely organized and structured system achieving
maximum efficiency. There is a network of sampling stations to
check the quality of the water and assure the maintenance of standards for each section of the river in response to its defined use. While
nobody claims that the charges represent the actual costs to the
last pfennig, they are eminently workable, and serve as incentives
to individual manufacturers to reduce pollution loads and as re-
minders that waste disposal costs are a part of production expenses.
Only waste producers pay for the maintenance of water quality;
the downstream water users are not charged for the benefits that
they receive. As a result of these efforts, one tributary river bed
is used as a controlled sewer, while 60,000 bathers daily may be
swimming in rivers at other locations within the region.

The polluters have the option to build their own treatment facilities,
thus avoiding the effluent charges. Yet it is an indication of the
efficiency of the entire system that only in a very few minor and
unique instances has this option been exercised. A considerable portion of the treatment costs are recouped through the recovery of
by-products and the sale of purified water.

Recent efforts to reverse the accelerating pollution of Lake
Michigan can also be noted. While many believe that Lake Erie
has passed the point of no return in eutrophication, a conference of
pollution control agencies representing the Federal Government and
four states[10] came to the conclusion that positive remedial action is
still possible for Lake Michigan, although the total cost may approach
billions of dollars. Inadequate treatment of industrial and municipal
wastes, combination sanitary-storm sewers, dumping of material from
harbor dredging, wastes from water craft, infusion of phosphates and
nitrogen, and the teeming population of alewives (a trash fish) were
identified as the primary causes. Technical solutions, research activities, and monitoring systems have been suggested, but it remains

[10] "Pollution Fought in Lake Michigan." *The New York Times,* February
11, 1968.

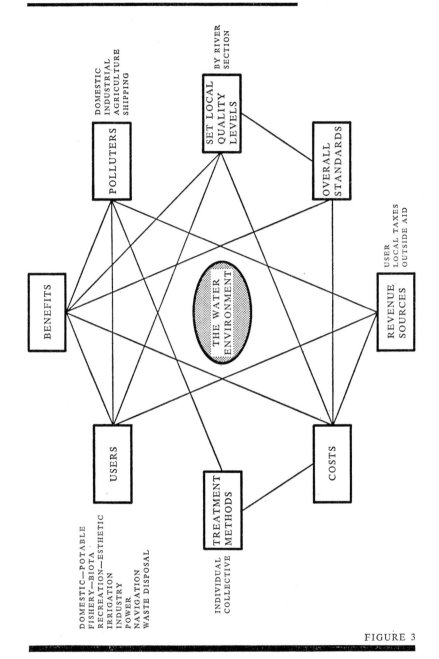

FIGURE 3

to be seen whether financial resources can be marshaled and administrative cooperation achieved among the various agencies involved. And whether this will be done in time.

TOWARD A COMPREHENSIVE MODEL

The following section will be devoted to the conceptual description of the structure for a model which attempts to include a rather broad array of pertinent aspects of water pollution and could serve, after further and more precise development, as the basis for a management-planning system of a water basin. (Most of the elements and their broad linkages are indicated in Fig. 3.) Such a model differs greatly from those which have appeared recently in the environmental control field having particular orientations and emphases: economic models described before or mathematical algorithms for quality prediction.[11]

The various types of polluters can be grouped in four classes, each having unique characteristics:

1. Domestic: low volume discharges at scattered locations, but in a fixed position where the individual discharges can be collected and conducted through one or a few points.
2. Industrial: high volume discharges at scattered locations with varied sewage characteristics; unified collection is not always possible or advisable.
3. Agriculture: run-off from fields which carries inorganic fertilizer with it; no collection or flow control is possible.
4. Shipping: discharges by vessels on navigable waterways of domestic-type sewage, garbage, or oil.

The effluents generated by the above can be regarded as the input elements and have to be measured as to their "strength" and character.

The discharges are received by water bodies which form the actual resource system. The uses and purposes of most rivers and lakes are multiple, often conflicting, and generally will include most of the following:

---

[11] See, for example, A. S. Goodman and W. E. Dobbins, *Mathematical Model for Water Pollution Control Studies* (reference 44).

1. Potable water for human consumption.
2. Potable water for animal consumption (livestock watering).
3. Water as life medium for marine flora and fauna.
4. Water as a recreational asset (direct,[12] such as swimming; semi-direct, such as boating; and indirect, such as scenic beauty).
5. Water for agricultural use, principally irrigation.
6. Water as raw material or coolant in industry.
7. Water as power producer in hydroelectric facilities.
8. Water as supporting medium for ships and other commercial vessels.
9. Water as a sink for wastes.

In order for any water body to function adequately in satisfying any one of the above purposes, it must have a corresponding degree of purity—the list is ranked approximately by decreasing purity requirements, i.e., drinking water must be of the highest quality while wastes can be discharged in any type of water which still has some degree of fluidity. This last item has been included not simply because many rivers and lakes have been used so in the past (with dire consequences) or that this practice could be acceptable at many locations, but rather in recognition of the fact that water has a certain self-cleansing capability, and that no commercially feasible treatment process can hope to achieve complete purity.

There are two extreme positions that could be taken with respect to the user requirements. First, it could be said that the highest use (domestic consumption) has to be satisfied, and consequently all water should be of drinkable quality. This obviously is not an economical or reasonable solution, since only a small portion of all the available water is consumed internally by human beings and all the other users can be satisfied with lower quality which can be achieved at greatly reduced costs.

Secondly, it could be postulated that each individual user is responsible for attaining and paying for the level of water purity that he desires. This approach unfortunately does not work, as evidenced by any number of rivers left unprotected against the abuses by waste generators—visual beauty and fishlife are the first to suffer

---

[12] Bodily contact with water.

since no private individual or firm feels directly responsible for them. Furthermore, the treatment of polluted water for any particular user may be considerably more expensive than removing the pollutants before they are discharged upstream; however, the waste producer has no economic incentive to do so voluntarily. The public has no choice but to assume the responsibility in protecting its members against unwarranted abuses by other members. The conclusion seems to be then that each waste generator should remove, or pay for the removal of, at least that portion of his pollutants which will have an adverse effect on somebody else and exceeds generally acceptable levels.

The last part of the previous statement is the most difficult aspect of environmental quality management. It recognizes by implication that everybody has a right to appropriate a portion of the natural purification capacity of water and air for his wastes which are produced as by-products of legitimate activities; yet the aggregate result of everybody taking advantage of this aspect cannot be allowed to reduce the standards of purity below defined levels.

This brings up the next point: environmental quality standards. In order to achieve an equitable and workable system, a control and measuring mechanism must be introduced. Since at the present a complete economic balance of costs and benefits for all users is not really feasible, a more or less arbitrarily defined set of standards[13] may serve the purpose quite well. It could even be suggested that, if and when precise economic calculations become practical, public demand for a level of visual quality with respect to rivers and lakes may still be the critical consideration, or at least the foundation on which details of criteria can be built upon.

One of the fundamental problems in formulating a rational and quantitative model of waste control is the lack of full understanding relating specific pollutants to their detrimental effects. The work is further complicated by the fact that usually a multitude of waste sources make their various contributions which intermix, decay at varying rates, and may even acquire new harmful characteristics if they are combined with other materials. The model must very definitely incorporate both a space and a time dimension to reflect

[13] See Chapter 5 and Appendix C.

adequately the dynamic behavior of pollutants in a liquid medium. But such variations are not only observable with respect to the wastes; the environment itself, or its absorption capacity, is greatly influenced by changing climatic and hydrological conditions. All these aspects are not yet fully researched.

Consequently, neither costs nor benefits of control work can be expressed in precise economic terms to achieve the best allocation of resources. Decisions at the present time have to be made on a somewhat subjective, if not political, basis.

The execution of the model can thus be envisioned in its actual operation as a determination, river section by river section, of desired quality standards (stream standards) as the thresholds which are not to be exceeded by pollution. These levels will be established in response to the dominant purposes of each river segment but will not be high enough, most likely, to satisfy all users. For example, the standards may specify a purity level which allows marine life to flourish but does not reach drinking quality. Any municipality on that stretch of river intending to use the water as the source of its water supply will have to be responsible for further treatment at the intake to satisfy its own requirements. But this will not be an excessive cost because of the high degree of purity already available.

The standards are to be set according to the specific uses of the river segment under consideration and also recognizing any applicable overall state or national policies.

The levels can only be maintained by careful surveillance and control of discharges, taking into account the self-purifying capacity of the river. Thus each potential polluter will have to meet the permissible maximum strength level of the discharge (effluent standards) before the wastes can be allowed to enter the waterway. The effluent standard differs from the river or stream standard by the amount of the direct and immediate self-purifying and dilution capacity of the receiving body of water. The discharge, which under no circumstances may have a greater state of pollution than the effluent standard, is to be upgraded through natural or artificial means to the river standard before it can affect any potential water user. If the wastes are stronger than the effluent standard permits, a treatment facility between the outfall pipe from a waste producer and the river, lake, or sea is needed. In order to achieve reliable operational results, a precise understanding of the biochemical performance of the river is, of course, a prerequisite to the establishment of proper standards and volume apportionments. Continuous monitoring—tuning of the system—will also be required.

All the above brings us back to the means and methods of treating the raw effluent to acceptable levels before discharge. The primary question here is again one of administration. Should this be the responsibility of, and should it be paid for by, the individual polluter or the community at large? The answer, which is still somewhat preliminary, would appear to be that the treatment of domestic waste is properly the responsibility of the municipality, and the expenses can be charged against general tax revenues or special uniform fees as a public service. Industries, on the other hand, create wastes as part of profit-making activities and, therefore, should be responsible for their neutralization. Faced with enforced regulations against excessively strong discharges, factories can solve the problem in one of several ways: either build their own treatment facilities or pay their proper share in a joint effort by several establishments or pay for the use of public facilities.

EXAMPLES OF POLLUTION IMPACT

Any number of examples can be given illustrating the great variety and complex interlinkages of pollution effects on the local economic and ecological situations. Such descriptive analyses can also provide the basis for an eventual quantitative cost-benefit determination for any particular watershed.

For instance, commercial fishing is a clear and measurable economic activity which can be destroyed or impaired by several consequences of water pollution. These include direct poisoning through toxic materials and pesticides, depletion of dissolved oxygen through biochemical reactions, silting and sedimentation of spawning grounds, detrimental effect of pollutants on the taste of fish, thereby reducing their commercial value, danger of absorption and carriage of pathogenic bacteria, and interference in marine life behavior through thermal and chemical changes. All the above have to be evaluated with respect to different species of fish which have greater or lesser tolerances to any one of these items. Furthermore, any precise economic analysis of commercial fishing will be complicated by the fact that fish may swim long distances from one watershed area to another, which means that the benefits of protecting the spawning grounds at considerable expense may be reaped by a different region or even a different country.

Nor can the importance of recreational fishing be neglected, although such benefits are not easily expressed in terms of dollars. This consideration leads to another economic aspect of pollution—somewhat more easily measurable, particularly under a crisis situation—which is water purity as a basic resource in the tourist industry. A number of famous resort areas, among them Honolulu, Puerto Rico, Nassau, and other Carribean islands, stand currently in great danger of curtailing their primary source of income by their own negligence manifested through beach pollution. At several locations in developing countries this is an asset which has been lost already before it could be exploited.

Another interesting network of meshed cause and effect relationships can be identified within the use of water for irrigation. To begin with, river flow volumes and their dilution capacity of liquid wastes are reduced through the diversion of water for agricultural purposes, and this happens usually during the hot months when volumes are low anyway and biochemical actions are intensified.

A great portion of the water that is spread on the fields evaporates, thereby raising the relative mineral content of the overflow. Salinity is increased further through the wash-off of artificial fertilizer. The water finds its way back to surface channels or contributes to the ground water. This progressive increase in salinity cannot be removed by cheap conventional methods; the economic impact is manifold: greater costs for drinking water purification, interference with marine biota, unsuitability for certain industrial processes,[14]

---

[14] Various industries can tolerate certain levels of pollution in process water, but a number of manufacturing activities cannot accept specific pollutants:
steel rolling—no chlorides
paper and pulp—no iron, manganese, or carbon dioxide
boiler-feed water—no corrosive or scale-forming chemicals, no biological materials
cooling water—no heat, no corrosive or scale-forming chemicals, etc.

and eventual deterioration to a point where the water becomes unusable even for further irrigation. This last aspect, for example, is creating international complications between Mexico and United States on the Colorado River.

SUGGESTED RESEARCH

Public opinion survey as to what levels of environmental quality are desired and what costs will be tolerated.

Precise work toward a watershed model relating pollution control and waste management features to economic considerations and other aspects of water use:

identification of waste generators and their waste contributions;

setting of objectives and criteria;

definition of economic and social cost of pollution;

identification of benefits;

evaluation of waste reutilization possibilities;

proposal of an administrative structure for cost allocation;

assignment of control and regulatory responsibilities;

development of feedback mechanisms and effective monitoring systems;

structuring of a continuous evaluation system allowing flexibility in operations.

Definition of the types of data required under a large-scale management system; investigation of methods of data collection and analysis.

3

SOURCES AND TYPES
OF POLLUTANTS

STUDIES AND MEASURES

In the analysis or design of a specific liquid waste disposal system, the single most important parameter is unquestionably the total volume of sewage generated by the community—today and during the useful life of the collection and treatment facilities. The physical dimensions of all the elements of the system are set by this measure.

It has been estimated [1] that the average rate of water consumption in cities and towns in the United States for all urban purposes is currently 155 gallons per capita per day (gcd). This figure, while useful as a general approximation, cannot, however, be applied directly as a sewage flow rate to any given municipality without adjustments. In the first place, there has been a long historical trend toward higher per capita use of water[2] which will continue unless certain restrictive modifications, as indicated later, are introduced. Secondly, each locality has unique characteristics which influence its per capita rates. The most important of these are industrial water use

[1] By the U.S. Geological Survey as reported in *Civil Engineering*, August 1967, p. 29.
[2] The trend and future forecast, according to the National Water Institute, is the following:

| 1900 | 50 gcd | 1960 | 150 gcd |
| 1940 | 122 | 1975 | 165 |

In addition to these urban demands, water use in farming is expected to grow from 766 gcd in 1960 to 821 in 1975, and for major separate industrial uses from 849 gcd to 1,193 in the same period.

and waste generation, which do not always return to the public sewers. Domestic use alone accounts for only about one third of the 155 gallons mentioned above. The first purpose of this chapter is to discuss the various factors that demand a careful and reasoned approach to volume estimates.

The other facet of basic inventory is the quality of sewage generated or, more properly, the degree of pollution of the discharged wastes. This characteristic not only fixes the internal design of treatment plants but is the prime factor affecting the environmental quality of the entire region. Here, too, distinctions have to be made among domestic sewage, various industrial effluents, and a number of other pollutant sources which have become critical recently, such as street wash-off, inorganic fertilizers, and thermal discharges.

Sanitary engineers are well aware of the design impact of variable sewage amounts and quality, yet their actual study and design methods have often been quite mechanistic. Occasionally such work has been limited to a filling in of the zoning envelope with maximum permitted population and multiplying the results by a selected per capita rate. This is not due to any technical negligence or lack of competence but rather to the usual uncertainty of anticipated future conditions in any particular municipality which obviates precise engineering decisions.

It can be suggested that planners, through their precise community studies and forecasts and through the use of various development controls, can give a stronger base for the estimate of future utility consumption rates and thereby help achieve a greater return per dollar in public works investment. Technical studies, traditionally regarded as the exclusive responsibility of the sanitary engineer, which set environmental standards, estimate future sewage generation volumes, and analyze waste quality and means of treatment require the direct participation of the urban planner to introduce the other related community building aspects which have a potential bearing on liquid waste disposal systems.

DOMESTIC SEWAGE

QUANTITY. The amount of domestic sewage generated within a community can be simply defined as the amount of water consumption minus losses and plus additions. For practical use, however, further elaboration of this statement is badly needed.

Recorded water consumption, which ranges anywhere from 90 to over 200 gcd for cities in the United States,[3] includes, in addition to domestic use, industrial, commercial and public demands as well as unaccounted losses (leakage) in water distribution pipes. If actual water consumption records exist for any study area, they would, of course, represent the strongest base for further estimates and projections. In the absence of such local figures, the absolute minimum domestic water consumption can be set at approximately 30 gcd under our present sanitary standards. This figure represents the amount that a human being actually consumes for his personal use. While troops on forced march can apparently survive with ¼ gcd under reasonable temperatures, flushing a toilet requires about 6 gallons of water and taking a shower 20 gallons or more. Thus 50 gcd is a more reasonable figure, especially considering that some unavoidable wastage has to be included. It is interesting to note that almost one half of this amount is not consumed in food or drink or used for bathing, but is rather discharged as a medium for carrying wastes.[4] Unless this water can be reclaimed later or the supply itself is plentiful and cheap, this is clearly a wasteful practice. Therefore, in regions of critical water shortage three modifications can be introduced:

1. use of inferior quality water for toilets (this requires, of course, a dual plumbing system);
2. use of waste disposal systems which require a minimum amount of water, such as the vacuum system developed in Sweden which uses only about one liter of water per flushing; and
3. the complete elimination of water as a waste carrying vehicle from the dwelling, and the development of chemical disposal systems or packaged collection networks.

[3] See pp. 18–03 and 18–04 in *American Civil Engineering Practice* by R. W. Abbett (New York: John Wiley, 1956).

[4] According to a 1964 study by the U.S. Geological Survey, the percentage breakdown is the following:

Flushing toilets	41 per cent	General household	
Washing and bathing	37	cleansing	3 per cent
Kitchen use	6	Watering the	
Drinking water	5	garden	3
Washing clothes	4	Washing the car	1

Domestic water consumption for each locality, in turn, is affected by climate, extent, and availability of sewers, presence of sink garbage grinders and washing machines, use of air conditioners, standard of living (economic level),[5] cost of water, quality of water, metering of water, pressure in pipes, and other factors which either increase or decrease the average rates and which are extremely difficult to predict precisely.[6]

Next, losses have to be subtracted. These include flows which do not return to sanitary sewers after use—lawn sprinkling, car washing, street cleaning, fire fighting—again adding up to an uncertain amount, subject to fluctuations. Usually, however, it is assumed that such losses are made up by sewage additions which do not come from the recorded municipal water supply, such as private wells.

Finally, sewer pipes usually receive water by infiltration through cracks or loose joints which can contribute large volumes to the flow in mains and treatment plants. While this amount is completely unpredictable, design studies include a standard allowance, such as, for example, 2,000 gallons per acre or 10,000 gallons per mile of sewer per day.[7]

All the above has referred to the flow for an average annual day. For actual design purposes, however, three cyclic variations have to be accounted for:

1. *Seasonal:* High daily volumes during the hot months with water being consumed for bathing, lawn watering, air conditioning, etc., and secondary peaks during very cold months when water is often left running to prevent pipe freezing.

2. *Daily:* Low water use during Sundays and heavy washing on Mondays.

---

[5] Or a "level of living index" as used in recent UN work.

[6] More specific information about the estimates of sewage quantity than is included in this work can be found in the following publications: *Design and Construction of Sanitary and Storm Sewers* (WPCF Manual No. 9) Chapter III (reference 66); R. W. Abbett, *American Civil Engineering Practice,* Section 18, Chapter 1, and Section 19, Chapter 2 (reference 86); M. F. Fair, et al., *Water Supply and Wastewater Removal,* Chapter 5 (reference 34); E. E. Seelye, *Design,* pp. 20–02 and 19–01 (references 102 and 103); H. E. Babbit, and E. R. Baumann, *Sewerage and Sewage Treatment* (reference 6); *Manual of Septic Tank Practice* (USPHS) pp. 36–39 (reference 133).

[7] The figures used range from 1,200 to 36,000 gpd per mile.

3. *Hourly:* High volume flows during morning hours with a secondary peak in early evening.[8]

For obvious health and esthetic reasons, sewer systems must be designed so that possible pipe overflows are completely eliminated. Consequently, the network must accommodate the flow of the heaviest hour of the heaviest day of the heaviest month of the year with the largest population within the design period. Without giving here the exact ratios and mathematical procedures,[9] the maximum hourly volume may represent three times the average annual rate for a locality, to which the amount contributed by infiltration must be still added.

Sewers must also be designed for the minimum flow—to assure that there will be an adequate volume and velocity of flow in the pipes to prevent settling out of suspended material which would clog up the lines or create septic conditions.

To summarize, the determination of future liquid waste flows, domestic or other, should be a carefully structured research procedure which builds up estimates starting with basic individual water consumption and modifying these rates according to local conditions and foreseeable future changes. This is an involved task, often hindered by lack of reliable data, but it is the only method defensible in the long run. Other approaches, such as the use of experience in "similar" communities, will give results which may be regarded as reasonable approximations, but will not be able to cope satisfactorily with the future projection aspects. A careful diagnostic and quantitative modeling of tomorrow's sanitary needs for a specific community may be more valuable in a practical sense than trying to extrapolate the past experience of a neighboring municipality. Even though the final results may be based on pyramided assumptions, a permanent and rational study structure will have been created within which dynamic modifications can be made as better information becomes available.

It should not be assumed that the preceding determination of flow quantities is only of interest to the sanitary engineer who is

---

[8] It has also been observed that there may be sharp but short peaks of sewage flow every hour and half hour during the evening—times when commercials come on on television. As a matter of fact, measurements of water pressure fluctuations have been taken by some organizations to test the effectiveness of commercials.

[9] See the aforementioned sanitary engineering references.

concerned with the detailed design and sizing of installations. The same calculations provide also the basic variables that contribute to the understanding of a community and its functional behavior, that establish the required scope of public services, and that eventually influence locational decisions regarding urban activities. As such, they constitute one of the first steps in a chain of planning studies.

QUALITY. The precise and detailed composition of domestic sewage will be of little interest to an urban planner. The liquid is an extremely complex chemical, biological, and physical mixture of various components (pollutants) carried by water. These materials can be classified into several groups, each having a particular impact on water quality and requiring special purification methods for its removal.

Most commonly the distinction is made between inorganic and organic material, the latter being regarded as the principal, if not the only, offender. This, however, is an oversimplification and, to achieve efficiency and reliability in water pollution control, a more detailed listing according to the physical state of the material is called for:

1. Floating debris and large pieces of material, usually organic in nature, are the most visible of pollutants and ones which cannot be readily reduced by natural biochemical action because of their size. However, their removal is easily accomplished by screens at the beginning of the treatment process and by skimmers within the plant itself. This collected material has to be handled further as solid refuse.

2. Suspended inorganic material, such as sand or grit, which again is readily removed by settling action and can be disposed as an inert and inoffensive material. The only problems that it can create are the silting up of water channels and the internal abrasion of pipes and machinery.

3. Dissolved inorganic materials, such as various salts and chemicals, which were regarded until recently as harmless ingredients and which may pass through the standard biochemical processes largely unchanged. They can seriously impair water quality for domestic consumption or industrial use, and can upset the ecological balance (biological feeding cycle) in receiving bodies of water.[10]

[10] See Inorganic Fertilizer, p. 47 for a discussion of the more recent approaches to the problem.

4. Suspended, colloidal, or dissolved organic material in an unstable form subject to biochemical action (oxidation, digestion, decomposition, and putrefaction) which, through the removal of oxygen from water and the accompanying creation of septic conditions, results in pollution as it is commonly understood. (Detergents and other foaming materials are also included in this class, although they present unique problems. The same can be said about toxic materials.)

5. Bacteria and other disease carrying micro-organisms—potentially the most dangerous components of sewage representing the original reason for urban sanitation control, but easily removed through direct disinfection.

The one characteristic of sewage that is not always adequately emphasized is that all the solids (or pollutants) together represent less than 0.1 per cent of the total weight. In other words, sewage is primarily water which has some nasty, but low volume additions.

The approximate breakdown of the various solids by amount in regular domestic sewage is shown in the following table[11] expressed as parts per million:

Suspended solids		300 ppm
Settling		
Organic	100	
Inorganic	50	
Suspended colloidal		
Organic	100	
Inorganic	50	
Dissolved solids		500
Dissolved colloidal		
Organic	40	
Inorganic	10	
Dissolved crystalloidal		
Organic	160	
Inorganic	290	
Total solids		800 ppm

[11] Metcalf & Eddy in *American Civil Engineering Practice*, pp. 19–18 (reference 86).

Wide variations, however, are possible in the composition and strength of domestic sewage, usually reflecting sanitary and food preparation habits of the population, as well as seasons of the year, presence of home garbage grinders, relative amount of diluting water, and age of sewage.

A number of standard tests and measurements of water quality have been developed to describe precisely the level of pollution found at any location at any time. The most important of these is the biochemical oxygen demand (B.O.D.) which can be defined as the amount of oxygen that is needed by any unit volume of sewage or polluted water to oxidize all organic material within it; this thereby restores conditions where any further addition of oxygen would be retained as dissolved oxygen available to fishlife and aquatic organisms. This *negative* measure (i.e., a deficiency) is usually expressed in pounds of oxygen used up on incubation of a water sample for 5 days at 20°C, and it is the most widely used descriptor of pollution. For example, any value of B.O.D. above zero indicates pollution, i.e., that state where no free dissolved oxygen is found in the water. The efficacy of various sewage treatment processes is usually measured as a percentage of B.O.D. removal.

While the above measurement is particularly applicable to sewage or effluent, the corresponding quality indicator for rivers and lakes, i.e., relatively unpolluted water, is the amount of dissolved oxygen —the reverse of B.O.D.

The impact of organic pollutant shock loading on a water environment is shown in Fig. 4 which represents the typical oxygen curve for a flowing river or a stationary body of water. The effect is twofold: The organic material represents a new food source which immediately allows an expansion of the biological communities of the lower forms of animals, and this in turn fosters growth of fishlife. At the same time, the organic pollutants undergoing biochemical reduction processes remove the free oxygen which causes a progressive suffocation of the higher animal forms and results in a spectacular increase in those bacteria which can tolerate septic conditions.

Sooner or later, depending largely upon the turbulence of the water, oxygen is reabsorbed and dissolved in the water through its sur-

EFFECT OF ORGANIC POLLUTANTS

ON WATER CONDITIONS

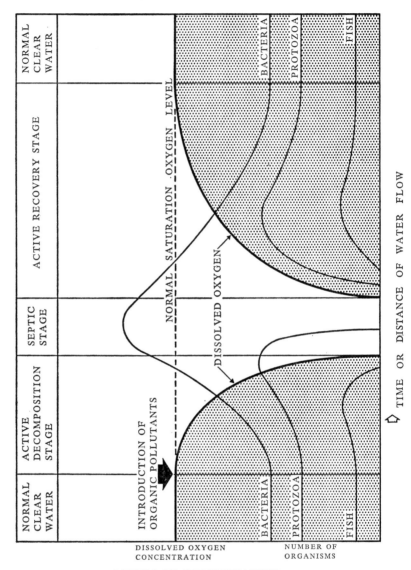

LEVELS OF CONCENTRATION

FIGURE 4

face, gradually neutralizing the pollutants and then rebuilding the oxygen levels to a normal saturation point. The animal life, with a certain time-lag, recovers too until the original dynamic equilibrium is reached again.

Other fundamental and often used measures of water quality are suspended solids (organic) and chlorine demand. The first is a simple expression of the amount of pollutants generated (as pounds per capita per day) or found in any given sewage (as pounds per unit volume). The second indicator measures the amount of chlorine required to render harmless all pathogenic bacteria within any type of sewage (expressed as pounds per capita per day).

Several other measurements of quality are available to test conditions under special purpose applications. They include such determinations as ammonia content, pH (acidity and alkalinity) levels, temperature, and salinity.[12]

In summary, the components of water pollution can be listed as the following elements and characteristics:

B.O.D.	Phenols
Suspended solids	Hardness
Dissolved solids	Color
Detergents	pH
Toxic materials	Temperature

To give a practical example related to the material discussed so far in this chapter, a study by the Texas State Department of Health[13] indicates that various state health departments use figures which range for total sewage volume from 150 to 40 gcd, for biochemical oxygen demand (B.O.D.) from 0.24 to 0.06 pounds per capita per day, and for suspended solids from 0.29 to 0.04 pounds per capita per day. The modal values were 100, 0.17, and 0.20, respectively.

More realistic values would be 100, 0.20, and 0.25, respectively, which are somewhat higher than presently used standards, reflecting the continuing upward trend in volumes.

[12] More precise descriptions of these tests can be found in WHO, *Water Pollution Control* (reference 161), pp. 17–20.

[13] N. W. Classen, "Per Capita Wastewater Contributions," Public Works, May 1967, pp. 81–83.

COMMERCIAL AND INDUSTRIAL WASTES

Even a superficial glance at some of the streams flowing through our cities should be enough to show the significant role that industry plays in the successful pollution of many of our waterways. There is no question that manufacturing is the *bête noire* in the field and, even if there may be some legitimate argument whether the amounts of waste from industry are greater or smaller than those from domestic sources, it is a fact that some untreated liquid discharges flowing from factories, because of their high level of concentration or toxicity, can thoroughly destroy the quality of any environment and even impair the capacity of treatment plants to deal with normal wastes. Industry is regarded by some as the source of about two-thirds of all contaminants pouring into our waterways. By 1970, its organic liquid waste contribution alone, excluding inorganic pollutants, will be equivalent to all municipal sewage. Or, to put it in another way, in 1960 industry was producing liquid wastes in an amount that could be generated by 160 million people. In 1970, if drastic abatement action is not undertaken, the population equivalent may reach 210 million.[14]

Manufacturers have started lately to construct their own pollution abatement works or to participate in control programs, more often than not in response to public pressure.

The problem is serious: specific countermeasures which can cope with many of the less standard effusions require the skills of experts such as the chemist, marine biologist, and industrial engineer. In the recent past, it was doubtful whether the planner's concrete participation could go much beyond such regulatory statements as: "no industrial wastes should be allowed to enter into municipal sewers that are stronger than regular domestic sewage." This very vague criterion was simply meant to exclude those wastes which would place an undue chemical or biological load on the standard treatment plants.

Today, with the ascendancy of the regional water resources management concept which attempts to analyze all potential pollution sources against all available treatment facilities and means of control,

[14] See "Industry Attacks Water Pollution" in *The New York Times* of October 14, 1965.

the responsibilities become broader, and a wider array of professionals need to be involved.

QUANTITY. Rule of thumb estimates of sewage flow from commercial areas range from 4,500 to more than 65,000 gpd per acre; the ones most often used are in the neighborhood of 30,000 to 40,000 gpd. These figures, like all general averages, have only a limited usefulness as preliminary approximations. For precise determination of flow rates, detailed analyses have to be made practically on an establishment by establishment basis utilizing observed and recorded amounts for specific activities.[15]

If few guidelines can be established for estimating flows from commercial facilities, no general statements whatsoever can be made with respect to industrial discharges. These range in volume and intensity from regular sanitary flows, generated by a few workers in an otherwise automated factory, to millions of gallons of noxious wastes pouring out from such complexes as steel foundries, paper mills, and chemical works.

The only general observation would be that each factory produces a unique type of waste, and that even two factories of a similar size and making the same product will quite likely generate different amounts and types of sewage. In any given industry, the variations will be caused by the differing characteristics of input materials, specific controls of the production processes and waste discharge methods, the level of technology employed in the plant, and the precise product mix of the manufacturing operation.

QUALITY. The character of any industrial discharge will depend not only on the type of industry, but also on the specific process employed, quality of supervision and control of emissions, as well as the size and organization of the establishment.[16]

[15] See Appendix A, *Sewage Generation Rates for Commercial and Public Establishments*. Many communities have adopted their own standards to estimate flows under various conditions. See also reference 141 for liquid wastes generated by various industries (pp. 95, 96).

[16] A great number of specialized reference works are available to anybody who would like to look into the question further, if for no other purpose than local policy determinations and evaluation of the potential danger presented to any environment by a new factory. Since each type of factory produces a

Even classification by types of pollutants becomes difficult since, in addition to the various components listed under domestic sewage, any number of other liquid or soluble materials may be discharged. These include the following broad groups:

1. Chemicals as by-products or overspill from various production processes. These compounds usually require special and precise chemical processes for neutralization or absorption.
2. Oil and grease which, if allowed to escape, can destroy equally well the biochemical processes of a treatment plant or a natural environment by coating all surfaces and thus stopping reaeration of water. Grease traps, provided they are maintained, are simple and effective corrective devices.
3. Toxic materials of various kinds which can kill fish and plant life even in extremely low concentrations. Factories generating such wastes must have reliable internal process controls, work under good maintenance and operational procedures, and be subject to continuous and precise monitoring of the effluent.
4. Radioactive substances which may result in a long-range adverse effect on all forms of life.
5. Heat from cooling water or production processes which again can change drastically the natural conditions found in rivers and lakes.

SPECIAL POLLUTANTS

In addition to the standard domestic and the various industrial wastes which are the primary pollutants, several other types or components have become recognized recently as serious offenders. These are certain forms of detergents, street wash-off, inorganic phosphates and nitrates, and high-temperature discharges. All of these, of course,

---

waste with unique characteristics which requires a tailormade treatment process, the search for references has to be on an industry basis. A staggering amount of such articles and publications dealing primarily with specific cases can be found in the technical press.

In addition to the industrial waste chapters found in all the standard sanitary engineering textbooks listed in the bibliography, there are also several general sources. Among these, the following two appear to be quite useful: C. F. Gurnham, *Industrial Wastewater Control* (reference 51); and W. Rudolfs, *Industrial Wastes* (reference 98).

have been in existence for some time, but their negative and over-whelming impact on a number of lakes and rivers has become spectacularly evident only within the last few years.[17]

DETERGENTS. In the 1950s, almost simultaneously at numerous locations in the United States as well as in several European countries, a new manifestation of water pollution appeared: huge banks of suds along rivers and creeks, foamy heads on drinking water drawn from private wells, and suds filling drain pipes in multistory buildings and escaping through sinks.[18]

This occurrence illustrated the power of advertising and speed of communications available today which, within a very short time, made many housewives aware of the supposedly beneficial qualities of a new type of synthetic detergent, an admittedly useful product. High production of suds was thought to be associated in the buyers' minds with cleaning capacity; therefore, detergents with spectacular foaming action were developed.

Without going into the chemistry and molecular structure of detergents, the simple fact was that the essential synthetic component of this detergent (alkyl benzene sulfonate (A.B.S.)) produced from cheap petroleum derivatives, could not be digested by bacteria found in rivers, lakes, and treatment plants. Consequently, the dissolved detergent traveled at full strength through filters and soil, and along rivers; it then foamed up again whenever it had a chance to concentrate. There has never been a better proof that disposal is not always accomplished by flushing something down a drain. Here was visual evidence of pollution which nobody could ignore.

The detergent industry's first reaction was to defend its product, and even to insist that it served as a tracer element indicating the presence of pollution from septic tank systems. This suggestion was not without merit, except that the synthetic detergents could travel

---

[17] Consequently, little material on them can be found in the standard textbooks, but there is an abundant crop of articles in the periodic literature describing the problems and giving case studies.

[18] During this period, the popular and technical press was filled with discussions of the problem. One such well-documented article appeared in *The New York Times*, April 23, 1962, on the problems on Long Island, "Water Pollution Arouses Suburbs."

much longer distances through soil than other pollutants, and that people really did not want to be shown that their water wells received effluent from their septic tanks.

To cut a long story short,[19] the industry in the United States, despite its first interesting defensive move, when faced with an adverse public reaction and threat of government action such as the outlawing of this type of detergent in West Germany, was able in 1965 to develop new forms of detergents which are biodegradable, i.e., can be digested by bacteria and thus destroyed.

A cardinal mistake had been made, and this oversight holds some lessons for the future. The experience shows how easily and suddenly a new, different, and widely used product can upset the already overloaded purification mechanism of the physical environment. It also points out that the manufacturers and responsible governmental agencies had neglected or had not thought of testing other characteristics of the product beyond its immediate use. The side effects in this case interfered with our well-being and esthetic sensibilities; next time they may threaten our very survival. Some pesticides could have such long-range impact.

The detergent interlude was an instance where nothing practical could be done through the collection and treatment systems; the remedy had to be applied at the source, the product itself. The only encouraging aspect of the entire case is the fact that our technology through the private enterprise system was able to find solutions swiftly, but a great amount of public concern and outcry was required.

STREET WASH-OFF. We are going through a long cycle in our attitude toward the handling of urban storm drainage, i.e., rain water which falls within the urban area and must be conducted away from streets and buildings.

The early sewer systems were all of the combined type[20] which simply poured together all waste fluids into the nearest body of water. As treatment plants were constructed at the outlet points to purify

---

[19] For a more complete case study see Chapter 12 in *Death of the Sweet Waters*, by D. E. Carr (reference 13).

[20] Almost 2,000 cities and towns in the United States, with a total population of about 60 million residents, are served currently by such systems.

the effluent before discharge, it was found, of course, that during heavy rain storms the plant capacity was exceeded by the flow, and large volumes of untreated, although diluted, sewage spilled over into waterways.[21]

Therefore, the switch in sanitary design was made to separate sewers: a dual system where sanitary flows are treated and storm flows are not. Yet, recent tests have shown that run-off which has washed city streets, especially after a long dry spell, can be just as offensive as sanitary sewage. This becomes rather obvious if one takes a close look at a city street. It collects fallout from the urban atmosphere, abrasion from pavements, tires, and vehicles, oil and gasoline spills, dog and bird droppings, and litter of all kinds.

The search for a solution here brings up several interesting possibilities which also illustrate the complex interlinkage of all aspects of urban operations.

The best approach would appear to be to institute a thorough street sweeping program, to reduce atmospheric pollution, and to control dog walking,[22] thereby reducing pollutants in the storm water. This, however, is a long-range, partial solution, and there is no reason why the natural cleaning action of rain water on streets should not be utilized. If cities or districts become covered by domes or other enclosures, the problem will change again. It can, however, be assumed that even then artificial street flushing will generate flows of dirty water, but these would be of sufficiently low volume to be absorbable by sanitary sewers.

Meanwhile, cities with combined sewers will have to continue using these systems, since it is completely unlikely that it would be economically feasible to construct separate networks in already developed areas. The costs are estimated at $30 to $50 billion nationwide, if everything were to be done today. Thus, modifications only

[21] It is to be noted that under extreme climatic conditions, caused by tropical rain storms when most of the annual precipitation occurs during a short period, storm drainage control must be approached quite differently since it is not feasible even to construct large enough sewers to accommodate the flash floods.

[22] It is incredible that with all our health codes and general attitude toward cleanliness and esthetic decency, we permit these completely primitive and offending practices toward the sanitary needs of household pets. The construction of dog toilets is not an unreasonable proposal.

can be suggested to eliminate the unacceptable practice of sewage overflow.

Large treatment plants could be built, but this too would not be practical since much of the time a large portion of the enlarged capacity would stand idle. A more reasonable suggestion is to construct impounding or detention basins which would collect excess flow during storms and then gradually empty these reservoirs through the treatment facility. Plant capacities would have to be increased since sewage would start to settle and decompose if kept in storage too long, but this enlargement would not have to be excessive. Such basins could be on the surface, as suggested for New York City, or in underground tunnels, as recently proposed for Chicago.

Under the latter project, large tunnels would be bored deep under the city, and all flow in excess of the capacity of the treatment plants would overspill into these underground reservoirs, perhaps generating electricity on the way down. Then, when the rain stops, the stored water would be pumped to the surface and back into the regular network leading to the treatment plants.

Another solution would be to insert a new, smaller pipe for sanitary flows, which would be treated at all times, within the existing combined sewers which invariably are of a large diameter since they must have adequate capacity to carry the volume of occasional cloudbursts; the normal domestic flow utilizes only a small portion of this capacity. The storm flow in the converted sewer would occupy the rest of the original pipe outside the sanitary line and could be conducted around the treatment plant. Construction costs for such modifications, including the reconnection of all house lines, would not be small, but they would be within reason. Furthermore, the initial storm flow carrying most of the dirt from city streets could still be passed through the treatment plant, if necessary.

A further refinement of this idea is explored by a project of the American Society of Civil Engineers;[23] this analyzes a system where each building would be equipped with a grinder and sewage pump forcing the wastes into a new pressure system leading to the treatment plant. The old combined sewers would be used for storm

[23] As reported in *Civil Engineering*, December 1967.

drainage; the new, very small diameter sanitary sewer could again be threaded through the existing conduits wherever feasible.

Other possibilities exist, for example, the addition of efficient, recently developed flocculants to the storm sewer overflows which could help remove and neutralize organic pollutants.

Built-up areas which have the newer separate sewer systems will have to work hard to find an acceptable solution; it seems that we may soon have to close the cycle and return to combined sewers in the dense city zones. In semirural and suburban districts, the storm flows will not be excessively polluted; separate sewers, therefore, will be the proper solution, provided that these areas remain at low density.

Since the outlets of storm drains are usually numerous and widely scattered in any community, their connection with interceptors, pumping stations, and a single treatment plant is completely unrealistic in most instances, nor is full-fledged treatment justified for storm water. The solution, therefore, probably lies in local screening and filtration at each sizable outlet, provided a cheap and automatic facility can be developed,[24] i.e., a simple screen or filter which does not require frequent cleaning and maintenance.

INORGANIC FERTILIZER. For many years the traditional approach toward sewage treatment has concentrated on the removal of organic material; the inorganic pollutants (such as nitrates and phosphates) were classified inert and thus harmless. However, they are nutrients or fertilizers of aquatic plant life.[25] This places them among the worst despoilers of water quality, since concentrations of these discharges have resulted in "blooms" of vegetation which remove oxygen from water, choke or poison water biota (including themselves), release odors, discolor water, and result in drifting and decaying masses of vegetation which interfere with all uses of the water bodies. Most

[24] The Rand Development Corporation is testing in Cleveland a filter which consists of a wire cage filled with coal. See *The New York Times,* August 28, 1966, "Engineers Doubt Clean-Up of Erie."

[25] The problem and possible solutions of phosphate pollution is discussed in a concise form by G. V. Levin in "The New Pollution," *Civil Engineering,* May 1967, pp. 68–71; in "More Air, More Sludge, Less Phosphates," *Engineering News-Record,* February 16, 1967; and by R. J. Sherwood in "A Synergistic Approach to Phosphorous Removal," *Civil Engineering,* May 1968, pp. 32–35.

deplorably, they hasten the natural eutrophication process turning lakes into marshes from a matter of centuries into years. The lakes of Erie and Geneva and numerous others, as well as rivers such as the Potomac, are currently in a critical condition due to excessive nitrate and phosphate loads.

The recent increase in fertilizer discharges can be traced to several causes: biological treatment processes release great amounts of the material, run-off from agricultural areas contributes a large share directly, the new biodegradable detergents are rich in phosphates, and there is the ever present problem of increasing population concentrations generating more wastes of all kinds.

The recognition of the problem has sparked research and testing of processes within the last five years that could cope with these effluents. Chemical neutralization, containment of algae growth in lagoons, distillation, filtration, ion exchange, electromechanical methods, removal by micro-organisms found in sewage, and other possibilities are currently under investigation. As with most aspects of sewage treatment, several methods can be used; the search is directed toward finding the most efficient and economical approach.

It is curious to note that the present efforts by sanitation experts are directed toward the elimination of these nutrients from the water environment as a liability; another group of scientists, concerned with the impending worldwide food crisis, is trying to develop methods useful in the cultivation of edible aquatic vegetation. The need for cooperation would seem to be indicated. This paradoxical situation points out again that each element and aspect of the environmental problem has to be regarded as a part of a larger system where, if it is analyzed and operated as a unit, net positive results are likely, whereas if each subsystem is handled separately, no constructive trade-offs are possible, and each may generate a deficit.

THERMAL POLLUTION. A very similar problem exists with respect to the discharge of high-temperature effluents in water bodies from power plants, factories, and other productive activities. Increase in temperature above the natural levels can and does alter the life situation in the water environment. This can result in drastic changes, expressed in fish kills, algae growth, and loss of biochemical purification capacity. There is also the economic problem of lost heat value through cooling water from power plants and heavy industry.

Recent evidence has indicated that this problem may become particularly severe with the expansion of nuclear power facilities which under present design configurations discharge particularly large amounts of hot water. The Connecticut River, Lake Michigan, the Columbia River Basin, and other places[26] are currently in such danger, and preventative action is called for. The simplest solution would be to construct air cooling towers or ponds to reduce water temperature before discharge; a more logical, although more complex, method would be to recapture the heat.

Yet, while thermal pollution can be just as destructive as any physical impurity, it can have a positive effect in a managed water basin system under controlled conditions. The heat could be used in fish or algae farming in sections set aside for that purpose,[27] provided that the ecological system needs and biological impacts are fully researched and understood; year-round swimming areas may also be created.

SUGGESTED RESEARCH

Preparation of precise guidelines to allow the calculation of domestic sewage volumes and characteristics for any community utilizing available socioeconomic measures as input variables.

Preparation of general guidelines for the estimation of commercial and industrial liquid wastes based on functional characteristics of the waste generators.

Investigation and development of an administrative mechanism under which operators of all non-residential uses would be legally responsible for the submission of information regarding the types

[26] B. Schorr, "Generating Plants Pose a 'Thermal Pollution' Threat to Rivers, Lakes," *The Wall Street Journal*, December 1, 1967.

[27] A large oyster farmer on Long Island Sound intends to purchase heated water from the local power company to extend his growing season to 10 months from the present 3 or 4 under natural conditions.

and amounts of wastes that their activities will produce and/or discharge within the foreseeable future.

Continuous research of the impact, control, and regulation of industrial and special wastes.

Development and establishment of simple and reliable measurement and monitoring procedures to determine instantaneously and continuously the pollution levels of sewage and natural water courses —as inputs for control devices and regulatory action.

Definition of a study structure (simulation model) for the quantity and strength estimation of all liquid wastes in a continuous process from all parts of the community at all times (present and future) to provide basic information for facility planning.

Planning and engineering study of the best methods to deal with surface run-off.

Investigation of waste disposal systems which do not rely on large volumes of water for waste carriage.

Coordinated nationwide research on the long-range effect of chemicals and high temperature discharges introduced in the natural environment.

Full-scale study of the long- and short-range effects of particular wastes on humans, animals, plants, and materials under varied but defined conditions.

4

TECHNOLOGICAL ASPECTS

The purpose of the following rather lengthy chapter is to review the various processes and engineering systems which are currently available in water pollution control. No attempt will be made to provide an exhaustive technical discussion—numerous standard sanitary text and reference books[1] provide that information—but rather to indicate the basic structure, requirements, implications, and results of the various possible solutions. The intention is to include here only those technical elements and details that are needed by the planner to decide questions of location, use, and density for an urban structure, and to do that in terms understandable to a non-engineer.

INDIVIDUAL SYSTEMS

Sanitary control in new subdivisions is usually regarded as being almost synonymous with septic tank systems,[2] i.e., individual systems serving each property separately and consisting of a septic tank proper, used to settle out the larger particles, and a drainage arrangement (tile fields or leaching pits) allowing the overflow liquid to seep into the ground.

[1] See references 6, 16, 33, 34, 53, 65, 66, 86, 97, 102, 103, and 113 (sanitary engineering texts); 29, 58, 61, 92, 99, and 108 (public health texts) at end of book.

[2] To be distinguished from cesspools (settlement and drainage taking place in single perforated tank), not acceptable under any conditions.

The two concepts of individual sewage disposal and suburban de-
tached homes, however, are not necessarily always exclusively linked.
Many subdivisions require communal systems, and septic tanks are
used in rural sanitation too. At the present time, about 50 million
people in the United States rely on septic tanks for their sanitary
services.

The technical information required in septic tank system design is
available in adequate supply;[3] the planning implications, in terms of
environmental sanitation and impact on community, require more investigation.

Since subdivision work is one of the few areas where planners can
exert direct authority and septic tank control is not a very involved
problem that would require the participation of a number of other
professionals as do other systems, this area demands careful attention. The planners' responsibility can be classified into several levels:
determination whether any area or parcel is suitable for individual
disposal, actual design of a system or checking of proposed layouts,
and the use of sanitary criteria as a developmental control.

The first item refers to the question raised earlier, selection of an
appropriate sewage disposal system. It should be recognized that
septic tanks are to be regarded only as a second-best solution permissible under certain well-defined conditions: (a) no existing community system within a reasonable distance and no prospects for one
within the foreseeable future; or (b) the presence of unique land

[3] The topic of septic tank design is well served by reference sources because
a single publication, *Manual of Septic Tank Practice*, by the United States
Public Health Service (reference 133) contains as much about the subject as
any planner or sanitation expert may wish to know and presents the information in a clear and organized way, making it directly usable for design and
review purposes. Many of the other good state or local manuals are largely
derived from this work.
There are a number of other sources which discuss septic tanks, but many
of them concentrate on the biochemical problems of anaerobic digestion. Of
practical value is a collection of papers from a World Health Organization
Seminar on Septic Tanks (reference 156). These look at the problem from
various sides, including an examination of systems servicing groups of houses.
A U.S. Department of Agriculture publication, *Farmstead Sewage and Refuse
Disposal* (reference 3), discusses rural sewage and refuse disposal and the
various methods available. In addition, the Yearbook of Agriculture, entitled
Water (reference 127), has a chapter on the same subject together with brief
articles on general pollution problems.

forms, such as extremely rough topography, which would make a collection network prohibitively expensive. If these conditions are satisfied, the next step is to investigate the subsoil characteristics. Septic tank operation is based on the natural liquid absorption and filtering capacity of the soil on the spot, and any volume of generated effluent requires a corresponding area or volume of suitable soil to receive it continuously over a long period. Consequently, districts where the soil is semi-permeable or impermeable (clay, hardpan) must be excluded as zones where septic tanks may be permitted. Likewise, a very thin good filtering layer (less than 4 feet deep below the discharge points) over an impermeable layer precludes the use of individual systems since the effluent will collect and run unfiltered for long distances over the watertight surface. If the area under question has special sanitary importance, such as being within a municipal watershed or recreational zone with numerous water courses, more careful analysis will be required.

Development of areas such as described above could then be allowed only if communal sewage systems are provided: collection networks with treatment plants. If, however, the conditions are not that critical and restrictive, the next step is to determine what maximum density can be permitted.

Several factors are involved here, and they can be discussed with respect to a single lot since this becomes the determining design element.

As stated before, the size of the required disposal area is a direct function of the amount of effluent, but it may have to be modified greatly according to the absorption characteristics of individual soils. For example, in sand which acts as a good and fast filter, the required area may be considerably less than for an equivalent house built upon clayey loam.

General soils information, outlining the location of soils' types can often be obtained from county-wide or other all-purpose soils surveys. This data, however, has to be translated into water absorption terms by a qualified geologist or engineer.[4] In many cases, especially where uncertainty exists, more detailed information will be required,

[4] See also *Soils and Land Use Planning,* papers presented at the ASPO Planning Conference, Philadelphia, Pa., April 1966.

and this can only be obtained through field spot checks with percolation tests.[5]

The calculated minimum absorption area for any given type of improvement, plus buffer strips along lot lines, buildings, and water courses, will then give the minimum permissible lot size. It should be superfluous to say that the lot sizes determined through the above procedure should correspond to the ones required by the zoning ordinance and should be recognized in the local subdivision regulations. The fact that this is not always so can lead to professional embarrassment for planners where health authorities can in effect veto decisions made on the basis of a superficial zoning ordinance.

That is, in many instances subdivisions have to be reviewed also by the local Department of Health which usually has greater experience in this matter and will be more strict with respect to septic tank proposals. To rely completely on this check is not a satisfactory planning and control procedure—the developmental ordinances must be realistic and reliable by themselves, and they must be coordinated with other applicable regulations.

The conclusion is thus very clear: there is a need for detailed consultation and cooperation among planners, geologists, and public health experts at the local level to achieve satisfactory environmental quality levels. This is rarely achieved at the present time.

The second responsibility of the planner may be direct design of septic tank systems or, most likely, the detailed review of plans submitted by the developer.

This design appears deceptively simple, and it is, provided that all site conditions, as described above, are optimal. In such cases, using the appropriate references, almost anybody can lay out a satisfactory system. And almost anybody is tempted to do this, which has led to a tremendous amount of failures, since the local conditions are only rarely excellent in all respects. A septic tank gone bad is not only a financial loss to the owner; it may be a health danger and an esthetic and olfactory nuisance to the community.

The primary duty of the planner as a reviewer is thus to recognize not only inadequate designs but also, and perhaps most importantly,

---

[5] See page 2 of *Manual of Septic Tank Practice* (reference 133).

to be aware of questionable local soil and ground water conditions which are not always readily apparent or which are purposely ignored. In such cases, field tests or the help of experts may be required. Furthermore, inspection during construction and approval is another safeguard worth considering.

The owner of a house with a septic tank should be made aware that maintenance costs for such system may be very high if something goes wrong; that the chances are that the seepage field cannot continue operating indefinitely; that, since individual water wells are usually found in subdivisions utilizing septic tanks, a direct pollution danger exists; and that, consequently, the resale value of this house is bound to be lower than that of a comparable property on a municipal line. According to some studies,[6] the difference may be $500 to $750 or more. The cost of providing public sewers for each house may only be one half to one quarter of the construction costs of bathrooms.

In any case, regular inspection and maintenance of each individual system is required to prevent a breakdown that may not be easily repairable. One of the greatest problems with septic tanks is the general absence of such programs; the home owner will usually only act when the system starts to collapse.

Again, the need for very strict local health and zoning ordinances is indicated and even other control mechanisms, such as Federal mortgage insurance, should be encouraged to look more carefully than they have at developments proposing to use septic tank disposal systems.

COLLECTION NETWORKS

Sewage disposal systems can be classified in two groups: on-site facilities and collective facilities. The first type includes septic tanks and other individual systems discussed in the previous sections as well as full-fledged treatment plants serving exclusively large installations, institutions, or activities. The pipe networks in these cases are minimal and usually under private management. The raw or partially treated effluent from on-site facilities may also be discharged

[6] J. A. Salvato (reference 100).

into collective lines for further purification and control instead of being disposed directly into the environment.

Community-wide sewerage systems consist of two basic parts: (1) a pipe network which serves to collect the flow of used water and convey it to a point of discharge where (2) a treatment plant is, or should be, located to remove varying percentages of the pollutants before allowing the water to enter waterways.

The collection network itself consists of pipe sections between manholes (for inspection and cleaning) within which the flow takes place by gravity. There are other elements for specific purposes, such as pumping stations to overcome topographic features, siphons to underpass other obstacles, flushing manholes to clean pipes periodically, lampholes for insertion of lights to inspect pipes, and, of course, house connections leading from individual buildings to the public sewage conduit.

The detailed design of these elements, as well as the size determination of pipes which involves calculations based on amounts of flow, desirable minimum and maximum velocity, slope, and pipe characteristics, is a purely engineering problem seeking to achieve the most economical and efficient solution to satisfy defined objectives. The planner has no contribution to make in the detailed design-calculation phase.

The layout of the network—its structure, service area, location of mains, and so forth—which precedes the above detailed design is, however, another matter. Regardless of the facts that this task too has been traditionally an engineering responsibility and that engineers should have the final word on the layout, there are a number of reasons why planners should be involved in the determination of the network pattern. The principal of these relates to the community-forming aspects of sewer service. In addition, the planner may be able to supply reasonable judgment as to which areas need service or which can be expected to grow in intensity thus requiring greater capacity pipes in the future. This information is not always available to the engineer. To achieve an organic and efficient layout, the designer—whoever he is—must have a "feel" for the land form, water drainage patterns, and physical obstacles, as well as their influence on the network.

The technical knowledge[7] required to participate in the conceptual layout of the system is not difficult to acquire. It is primarily a matter of understanding how the network operates and learning some design criteria and requirements, such as spacing between manholes, configuration of pipe linkages, maximum and minimum slopes, and feasibility of deep trenches.[8]

The on-the-site required technical information includes surface elevations (gradients), subsoil types, location of rock formations, and presence of ground water. The general criteria for the layout of the system are maximum economy in construction and material costs, minimum expenses for future maintenance and operation, and the servicing of all sewage generators with the least disturbance of urban activities during construction or thereafter.

A not insignificant additional benefit from the planner's attempt to participate in the design task will be that the knowledge and experience thus gained will enable him to evaluate in a more reliable way the potential for, and feasibility of, development of zones of the city and to judge the adequacy of any existing systems for the anticipated future loads, as discussed at a later point.

It is to be noted in passing that in this area of design, which has seen little change ever since municipal sewer lines have been built on a large scale, a few new approaches have been examined in recent years. One of these is the problem of combined sewers, discussed previously; the other is the use of curved alignments of pipes.

Standard practice demands that lines be straight between manholes for visual inspection and ease of cleaning (rodding through). This requirement creates a few inconveniences. For example, on a

---

[7] It is a singular fact that most sanitary engineering textbooks skip over this subject very lightly and do not provide all the guidance required—perhaps because the technical problems are not very involved, and the community building aspects are not of direct concern to sanitary specialists. All these references, however, do contain some information, but a certain amount of interpretation and consolidation may be needed by the reader. The most compact treatment can be found in the works by Fair and associates (reference 34), Seelye (reference 102), and Escritt (reference 33).

The manual by ASCE and WPCF on design of sewers (reference 66) represents the most thorough discussion of the topics involved. These range from quantity calculations to power requirements for pumping stations. The work, unfortunately, lacks even a single drawing of a typical layout, but it is strong in the details of appurtenances and other system elements.

[8] See Appendix E.

curved street with curbs, pavement, and other utilities all running parallel and concentric, the sewer lines cut across all other alignments by attempting to go around a circle with straight line segments. There is evidence that curved sewer lines with a reasonable radius are feasible because of the availability of modern, mechanized, and powerful cleaning apparatus.[9]

It has been estimated [10] that the collection network represents about three quarters of all the construction expenses of a sewerage system, or typically an expenditure of $200 per capita. In small communities about 5 miles of sewers are required to serve each 1,000 population, in larger cities, 3 miles per 1,000.

TREATMENT FACILITIES AND PROCESSES

The biological, chemical, or mechanical removal of impurities from domestic and industrial effluent before discharge—sewage treatment—is, in its microscopic scale, an extremely complex operation understandable only to a specialist.

For a very long time, until the end of the nineteenth century, raw sewage discharged from cities and communities had been absorbed by the water environment, diluted, and eventually purified through natural processes. This worked satisfactorily only where the receiving lakes, rivers, seas, and oceans had a very large dilution capacity and the effluent volumes were relatively small. Today such conditions are almost impossible to find anywhere in the settled portions of the world, and artificial treatment is required. There may be only a few isolated instances where the discharge of partially treated sewage in seas or oceans, not lakes and rivers, can be considered, provided that a number of criteria that assure safe disposal are met: outfall lines have to be very long; currents and tidal flows must be such that rapid mixing and diffusion takes place and the effluent is not washed back into the shore.

During the relatively short period when municipal treatment facilities have been built to any appreciable extent, several standard

[9] See the feasibility analysis in reference 31.

[10] C. H. Lawrence, "Economic Considerations for Sanitary Sewers," *Public Works,* March 1967, pp. 99–102.

processes have been developed and tested, and are now used almost universally. They are sedimentation, chemical precipitation, trickling filtration, and activated sludge treatment. All of them, with the possible exception of chemical precipitation, imitate the natural biochemical purification action that would take place in any body of water, but they speed it up by creating a suitable environment for the operation and they control it. These processes, packaged in a largely standard unit or tank, have not changed much during the last thirty years.

A municipal treatment plant consists of a chain of units hooked up to give a progressively cleaner effluent; each unit has a specific purpose: to cope with a particular pollutant or to improve the quality one step farther. The design of a treatment plant thus basically consists of the selection and arrangement of those unit processes which, in order to achieve a defined level of purity, would best be able to deal with the particular type of sewage generated in the community. Such design must recognize a number of other conditions: cost, character of receiving body of water, plant site limitations, size of operations, sludge disposal problems, and several others. The detailed engineering design involves, of course, the careful sizing of all elements according to the anticipated volumes.

Since even when working with standard elements a number of combinations are possible and precise calculations are required, this is a task for a specialist: a sanitary engineer. A planner cannot be expected to have more than a general understanding of the processes and how they fit together,[11] he should be able to recognize their planning implications and impact on the community, such as costs, location, and potential nuisance problems, and be aware of some new developments. The rest of this chapter will be devoted to these aspects.

PRIMARY TREATMENT. The standard sewage purification plant operation consists of two parts: primary and secondary treatment.

---

[11] Detailed descriptions and evaluations can be found in a number of sanitary engineering textbooks: references 16, 34, 53, 86, 97, 103, and 113. Beyond that, the professional periodic literature is rife with any number of articles and discussions which analyze and describe the various purification methods from all points of view; they can be located through the use of the Engineering Index.

The primary section utilizes mechanical processes and is thus able to remove only the larger floating, suspended, and undissolved particles. The first step is screening, which may be accomplished by one or a series of progressively finer screens. The screenings must be removed as solid wastes or handled by a comminutor which grinds up the material and returns it to the flow. This step is usually followed by a grit chamber, which is a simple rectangular tank with flow velocity controlled in such a way that the heavier inorganic particles (sand and grit) settle out, but the lighter, suspended organic material is carried along with the liquid. The next unit is a primary settling tank, which again operates on the basis of gravity alone: through-flow is slow enough for a considerable portion of the suspended particles to settle out and for scum to float to the top. This material is removed by mechanical scrapers and constitutes sludge which requires further attention, as will be seen later.

The primary process does about half the job,[12] it is largely effective only with respect to the readily visible pollutants and particulate matter. While there are a number of communities in the United States which still have no treatment facilities whatsoever, the greater portion of Manhattan Island among them, there is an even larger number of places which provide only primary treatment before chlorination and ultimate disposal. This can and does result in pollution of the receiving bodies of water and, therefore, secondary treatment as the next stage can almost always be justified. The rare situation where primary treatment alone would be satisfactory is perhaps a small community removed miles from all other settlements on a large turbulent river which is not used for water supply or recreation. But even then destruction of the aquatic environment is an ever present danger.

The relative utilization of various disposal methods, in terms of population served, in the United States is shown in Fig. 5.

SECONDARY TREATMENT. In secondary treatment the operations are biochemical in nature, i.e., bacteria react with the putrescible organic colloidal or dissolved material by absorption, digestion, oxidation, assimilation, or decomposition. The results of this activity are settle-

---

[12] See table *Efficiencies of Sewage Treatment Units,* Appendix B.

METHODS OF SEWAGE DISPOSAL
IN THE UNITED STATES

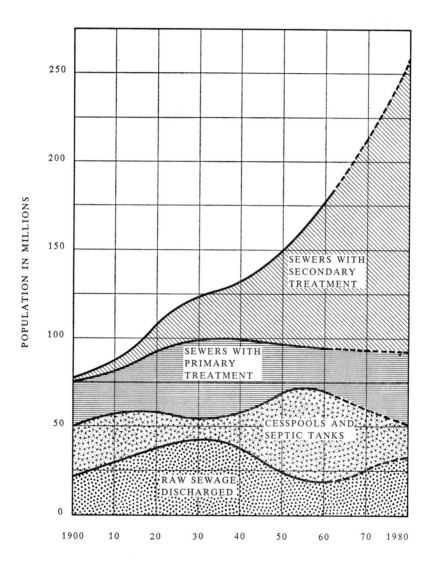

SOURCE. *INTERNATIONAL SCIENCE AND TECHNOLOGY*, MAY, 1965   FIGURE 5

able organic particles or inert mineral substances. The operation takes place in the presence of oxygen (aerobic) in the two processes most often used: trickling filters and activated sludge.

The first utilizes a bed of crushed stone over which the effluent from the primary stage is sprinkled, usually by means of rotating arms. The stones are covered by biological growths (slimes) which represent the active agents in the adsorption or reduction of the pollutants. Oxygen is supplied by air which can circulate between the stones or other filtering media. The products of this biochemical action are washed out and carried by the liquid to the next unit, which is a settling basin.

The activated sludge process accomplishes the same task in a completely wet environment. The flow enters into a longitudinal tank and is mixed with a certain amount of returned sludge from the final settling basin. This sludge is rich with biological growths (and thus activated, since it has gone through the process already. The particles and molecules in the raw sewage are adsorbed or otherwise acted upon by the flocs of sludge in suspension. Air is supplied through bubbling devices along the length of the tank. The settling tank after this unit removes the particles in a way similar to the primary settling tank. That portion of the sludge which is not returned must receive further treatment.

Any number of modifications and refinements can be introduced in the above two processes,[13] but, while such improvements can achieve greater degrees of purity, they do not change the basic operations.

For most communities, if they do not have other large settlements immediately downstream or if the receiving body of water is not used directly for drinking water, treatment achieving over 90 per cent purity is quite satisfactory, and the great bulk of treatment plants built in the United States employ either the trickling filter or activated sludge process. Since both are almost completely comparable as far as effluent quality is concerned, the selection of one or another for

[13] Such as multiple stages, high flow rates, combinations of units, different physical configurations, and controlled stepwise addition of effluents and materials.

a specific community is a rather difficult problem with no clear-cut guidelines possible because of variations in local conditions.

Generally, however, the activated sludge plant is characterized by greater compactness, thus less demand for land, lower initial construction costs but higher operational expenses than a trickling filter plant of the same capacity. The activated sludge plant requires also continuous supervision and control to regulate the process; whereas the trickling filter ordinarily needs only an intermittent check. Consequently, the first type of plant is usually found in large cities and metropolitan areas. They serve large districts and are of considerable size. The premium on space is one reason, and a large operation can justify trained personnel. Trickling filters, on the other hand, are most common in villages and cities of smaller size. Yet, there are enough exceptions to preclude making the above observations into reliable rules.

Very often the biological secondary processes can be reinforced by a chemical treatment unit, or this process may form the core of the plant by itself. This operation consists of the introduction of such chemicals as alum, lime, ferric chloride, or similar compounds in the screened effluent within a mixing basin where flocs are formed. In the next unit, which is a sedimentation tank, these large artificial particles settle out, removing a good portion of the suspended and dissolved organic material too. The load on the biological filters, which usually follow, is thus considerably reduced. If it is a complete chemical treatment plant by itself, the precipitation action can be intensified to achieve a desired level of purity, although some filtration of the effluent may still be required. Some of the problems which are present are the relatively high cost of the chemicals, the need for rather careful control of the process, and the difficulties in sludge digestion since it contains a high percentage of inorganic chemicals.

OTHER SECONDARY TREATMENT PROCESSES. In addition to the two widely used processes of trickling filtration and activated sludge, there are a few others that are or have been used rather extensively.

One of these is the Imhoff process which was most popular from about 1910 to 1925 and can still be found in operation in a number of small cities and villages, although today this system is very rarely utilized for new plants. It consists of a single tank within which settlement takes place, and the sediments are reduced through anaerobic digestion at the bottom of the tank. The operation is difficult to control, and the effluent is of low quality.

Another old process, which however shows signs of increased future use because of new refinements, is aerated lagoons.[14] The modern lagoon is a far cry from the primitive basins used in the past, which simply allowed sewage to settle and putrefy, thus creating a nuisance of considerable dimensions.

A distinction has to be made under present practice between oxidation ponds, which serve occasionally as adjuncts to regular treatment plants for further purification of the effluent and sewage, and stabilization lagoons which constitute the core of a special type of facility.

The process is inexpensive to operate, but it requires great amounts of land.[15] Little maintenance is needed, but the ponds present a visual liability and a potential source of odor. A further refinement of the concept is to introduce mechanical aerators to speed up the process. The lagoon then operates under aerobic and anaerobic conditions at different water levels, and the land requirement is reduced.

Even though stabilization lagoons reproduce most closely the natural purification action of lakes and rivers, their wide use for domestic sewage disposal is doubtful on a large scale. But there are hundreds of small communities, especially in the Midwest, which use them. Their great potential appears to be for industrial waste control at isolated locations, particularly because the lagoons have an impounding capacity which can even out the peaks of flow found in manufacturing operations.

SLUDGE DISPOSAL AND BY-PRODUCTS. The liquid effluent from these chains of units, after chlorination, is ready for discharge; the solid matter which has been distilled or otherwise removed—sludge—

---

[14] See "Sewage Lagoons and Man's Environment," by J. H. Svore in *Civil Engineering*, September 1964, pp. 54–56.

[15] One acre of surface for each 200 to 400 people; a 5–30 day detention period.

forms an active and greatly offensive concentrated slurry of pollutants. The most common method of rendering this material inoffensive is sludge digestion, i.e., anaerobic biochemical action aided by heat in a closed container. This results in a product of foul appearance but otherwise inert. The digested sludge, after dewatering, can be buried, burned, or used as fertilizer. Other more primitive sludge disposal methods can also be encountered, such as simple dumping, lagooning, or drying.

At this point, several observations about the possibility of recovering useful by-products from the treatment process appear to be in order. That is, the traditional view of sewage as a 100 per cent liability needs to be modified in recognizing that under certain conditions the retrieval of energy or marketable products may pay for a part of the treatment cost. Underlying this approach is the basic need for the conservation of resources of any kind and under all circumstances; there are also immediate and practical economic considerations.

The reuse of water will be discussed in a following section, but the removed solid matter too has useful properties. Unfortunately, in this country with our rather wasteful attitude toward resources, high labor costs, efficient industrial methods creating products from still abundant original resources, and the need for large-scale operations and marketing organizations, the recovery of waste materials, especially from sewage, has never been strictly necessary or profitable.

Yet, sewage sludge generates burnable gas during the digestion process, and the final dried material is an excellent fertilizer. But only a few treatment plants have gone as far as at least to utilize the gas for internal power production and heating; most others burn it off or simply let it escape. Likewise, because of the cheapness of artificial fertilizers and the relative absence of extensive farming activity near the large cities that generate the greatest amounts of sludge, the use of the final product of the treatment plant in a constructive way is extremely limited. Milwaukee, which markets its milorganite as a dry material in bags, is one of the few communities that appears to have achieved any measure of success in this area in the United States.

Another approach to accomplish the same aim would be the

pumping of wet sludge to nearby marginal lands for their gradual conversion to agricultural use. Feasibility studies have been started to investigate this possibility.[16]

It is to be noted that the potential benefits from a resource recovery program are twofold: it is not only the direct monetary return, but also the simple fact that in many of our dense urban areas space for dumping is rapidly being exhausted.

Several advanced sludge disposal methods are also being considered currently. For example, an experimental 2 million gpd plant utilizing gamma radiation will be put in operation in Chicago, which promises to allow easy dewatering, stabilization, and disinfection of sludge and to break down special substances like cyanides and phenols.

TERTIARY TREATMENT. In many of the densely urbanized sections of Europe it has been clear for some time now that secondary treatment alone is not adequate to preserve the necessary level of environmental quality, and that further "polishing" of the effluent is required. The same conclusions are also beginning to be reached at several locations in the United States. The provision of tertiary treatment is thus emerging currently as a practical consideration, rather than only a theoretical and experimental problem on a pilot plant basis.

Very briefly, the aim of tertiary treatment is to reach purity levels around 98 and 99 per cent of B.O.D. and suspended solids removal. To achieve this improvement of a few percentage points above the secondary treatment levels is, however, an expensive and complex undertaking for which a number of processes can be suggested but where there is no general consensus as to the best approach. Each locality has to select the method which appears to suit it best, and the catalogue of possibilities follows. A purity level of 100 per cent, of course, is also possible through distillation and extreme filtration, but it is not necessary, since none of the natural water courses are that pure nor is it economically feasible because of the skyrocketing costs at this level.

---

[16] Under a Public Health Service grant to the City of Chicago, as reported in *Civil Engineering*, September 1967. See also V. W. Bacon and F. E. Dalton, "Chicago Metro Sanitary District Makes No Little Plans," *Public Works*, November 1966, pp. 66–70, 140–42.

Some of the methods used will be familiar since they are nothing more than refined and improved secondary processes. For example, trickling filters and activated sludge units may be hooked up into multi-stage arrangements either of the same type or in a variety of mixed combinations.[17] Similarly, oxidation ponds and stabilization lagoons can be used for this purpose. Land application—intermittent irrigation of fields used for crop growing—is another simple but acreage-consuming approach. Recharge of ground water table through trenches[18] also comes under this classification.

Rapid sand filtration, practically identical with the method used for drinking water purification, gives extremely high effluent quality. The process consists of pumping the liquid from the secondary treatment units on top of a sand bed through which it is allowed to filter for collection underneath. The filter is backwashed regularly. Very similar results can be obtained by the use of mechanical micro-strainers—moving screens of a very fine mesh stainless steel fabric. Chemical precipitation can also be utilized at several points in the treatment sequence to achieve effluents in the 99 per cent quality range.

One of the most extensive tertiary treatment operations in the United States has been developed recently by the Metropolitan Sanitary District of Chicago. The experimental plant (Hanover) will use coagulation followed by rapid sand filters and will test the effluent for phosphate, organic material, and pathogenic bacteria removal. This pilot plant is one of several across the country currently being evaluated to develop advanced methods and procedures in liquid waste control.

NEW PROCESSES. In concluding this section on treatment processes, a number of recent developments and approaches which often represent basic departures from the traditional methods described previously deserve mention. Almost all of these are new inventions that

[17] A brief but thorough description of tertiary sewage treatment is provided by C. E. Keefer in two articles which appeared in *Public Works* (reference 68), together with examples and references. Also by D. G. Stephan in "Water Renovation—Some Advanced Treatment Processes," *Civil Engineering,* September 1965, pp. 46–49.

[18] See p. 72 on water reuse.

have not been completely tested, evaluated, or even described in the technical press.[19] Some of these processes may emerge as efficient replacements for the standard methods which, as was shown, leave much to be desired in several respects.

Some of these new processes are intended to replace the traditional methods entirely; others are designed to supplement the old units or give tertiary treatment.

An example of the first type is the so-called Zimmerman process which has been installed for regular use in several locations, among them Chicago;[20] Rye, New York; South Milwaukee, Wisconsin; Wausau, Wisconsin; Wheeling, West Virginia; and others. The method, which is beginning to compete with the conventional plants, utilizes a wet oxidation process, i.e., the organic material in liquid solution is burned in a pressurized container through the introduction of air. The ash settles out readily. Many of the treatment steps of the standard plant are thus combined in one unit. Furthermore, the operations require little space and are completely enclosed, thus producing no impact on the surrounding area. It is, however, a complex industrial operation requiring skilled control and external energy input.[21]

The new Calgon process[22] employs polymeric chemicals for coagulation and sedimentation (polyelectrolytical flocculation) and completes the treatment through granular activated carbon filters which retain the remaining suspended solids and adsorb dissolved organic contaminants. The company claims that this process will require only one tenth of the land, achieve a higher degree of purity,

---

[19] In addition to the specific references listed on the succeeding pages, several publications provide a general comparative picture of the various methods: reports originated in the R. A. Taft Sanitary Center, particularly their 999-WP Series (reference 74 and others), articles in *Public Works* (such as reference 68), and a great number of separate items in the *Journal of WPCF* (reference 46, for example). However, in most cases, these articles are too technical to be of much use to the planner, and very rarely do they attempt to place the various alternatives in the proper perspective as far as their utility and potential are concerned.

[20] So far the largest of its type, it has a capacity to serve a population of 2 million.

[21] Pressure of up to 2,000 pounds and temperature up to 600°F, although some of the exhaust heat can be recovered to drive generators.

[22] "Calgon Unveils Method for Treating Sewage at Much Lower Cost," *The Wall Street Journal,* February 7, 1967.

and cost about two thirds of the corresponding amounts for conventional plants since the carbon filters can be cleaned and reused. This and similar metal ion processes are reported to achieve good results in phosphate removal.

Other chemical and industrial firms are searching for better flocculating chemicals or filtering media[23] such as powdered coal or plastics. Mechanical operations, such as centrifugal separation,[24] are also tested, as are oxidation approaches. Direct incineration of sewage or sludge, despite its high costs, has received some attention as a special purpose method with a number of variants. Several other processes, which have been investigated in connection with sea water desalting, can be regarded as having a potential in the final purification of sewage too: heat distillation, freezing out of water, electrodialysis, foaming, and reverse osmosis. One more interesting possibility may be the use of enzymes to stimulate the reduction of organic pollutants into inert products.[25] But all of these are still in the laboratory stage.

It is apparent from a review of all this experimentation that the search is directed toward a more industrialized and chemical rather than the traditional biological approach in sewage treatment. Emphasis is placed on compactness, speed, and thoroughness in the purification operations, even if higher costs are incurred initially. This can be well justified because of the currently observable disappearance of open space in urban areas, the demand for a better environmental quality, and a gradually improving willingness on the part of the public to pay for it all.

PACKAGE PLANTS

In the 1950s, in response to the demand for treatment facilities to serve isolated small subdivisions, institutions, shopping centers, highway service areas, recreation facilities, or other activities which were not near any public sewerage systems, a number of sanitary equip-

[23] "Drive to Cut Pollution Scores Gains, Saves Money for Some Firms," *The Wall Street Journal*, May 4, 1962.
[24] "Fluo-Solids" process of Dorr-Olivers.
[25] "Tenderness in the Kitchen," *Time Magazine*, September 21, 1962.

ment manufacturers developed and placed on the market the so-called package plants.

They are factory-made compact units which are transportable and contain all the necessary equipment for sewage treatment. The various elements may be packaged into a single tank, or they may be bolted together in the field. Package plants are for all practical purposes miniaturized trickling filter or activated sludge units with built-in sludge digestion and chlorination capability; they are designed to operate with a minimum of supervision and control and can remove up to 90 per cent of the pollutants found in sewage.[26]

In order to achieve such semiautomation, the process is usually overdesigned, i.e., capacity calculations incorporate a considerable safety factor. Consequently, package plants have a relatively heavy power consumption, and they cannot compare in engineering efficiency with standard treatment plants under continuous control.

But this is not their purpose. Package plants can be regarded as filling the gap between simple individual septic tanks and the large-scale, custom-designed municipal treatment plants. For example, it is expected that several local systems will be built on Staten Island, New York City, in areas which are undergoing intensive development and are at the present far from the municipal network. The first such district will serve 1,200 homes on 140 acres and have a $400,000 treatment facility. When city interceptor lines become available, the local collectors will be connected to these, and the plant site will be used as a recreation area.

The capacities of the various systems on the market today, produced by some twenty manufacturers, range from units suitable for a few homes to plants able to deal with 500,000 gpd. Under ordinary suburban conditions, a 50-house development (or even 25, if the homes are expensive) is large enough to support economically a local collection network with a package treatment plant.

---

[26] Several articles in the December 1960 (p. 147), February 1961 (reference 57) (pp. 111–13), and April 1961 (pp. 111–13) issues of *Public Works* are devoted to the subject, and give descriptions and examples. An overall view of their use can be found in "Packaged Sewage Disposal Plants," *Progressive Architecture* (reference 123). The publication by the National Research Council, *Report on Individual Household Aerobic Sewage Treatment Systems* (reference 120) provides detailed technical information.

As with all new inventions, there was, and still is, some reluctance by various state and local health officials to allow their use. Generally speaking, they are now accepted by municipalities in New Jersey, Pennsylvania, and most Midwest states; other localities resist them through restrictive ordinances.

Although in most instances the experience has been completely satisfactory, precise controls of package plants are not out of place at all. Their capacities and types have to be selected carefully in line with anticipated loads, they do require regular inspection and maintenance, and they have to be screened and fenced in. And if a plant goes bad, there is a memorable although temporary olfactory impact on the surrounding area.

The plants are vulnerable to shock loadings—sharp increase in flow volumes—which may cause a large quantity discharge of solids in the effluent. Mechanical failures of the equipment can have the same result. Since continuous operator attention is not feasible nor can it be recommended because of the nature of the facility, several improvements have been suggested as safety precautions against intermittent plant upsets:[27] final sand filtration of a type that can operate automatically under all circumstances and duplication of vital equipment, such as air compressors. A buffer strip of 500 feet may also be advisable.

While package plants satisfy a very real need for an intermediate size environmental control facility, they also have several important planning features. The prime one is that they can serve as permanent facilities at isolated locations or can be regarded as interim improvements in a changing area. This is particularly applicable to a growing suburban area where developments will be scattered in the early phases but will require sanitary disposal facilities from the very beginning. Instead of building individual septic tanks that would have to be abandoned as a complete loss when densities and development coverage becomes intensive enough to demand municipal sewage collection networks and treatment plants, a much more rational policy would be to establish small service districts for each separate development with sewage collection lines and a package plant.

[27] G. Culp and S. Hansen, "Tertiary Treatment for Small Plants," *Public Works*, December 1967, pp. 82–85.

When the area reaches maturity, all the individual networks can be hooked up to interceptor sewers which will conduct the flow to a new large-scale municipal treatment plant. The individual package plants in most instances can be easily salvaged for reuse elsewhere. Needless to say, this is one obvious case where a realistic and precise master plan is absolutely indispensable in order to consolidate all the separate improvements into a single system at a future date. The advantages of time and space flexibility under such arrangement are rather clear.

An important additional advantage is that relatively low initial investment is required; this can be carried by the new home owners directly and does not demand a large expenditure by the municipality during the years when the revenue base has not yet developed. Package plants, because of their small size and because much of the equipment can be buried, present very limited visual and land use compatibility problems. They can be installed by a general contractor and do not require special expertise or skills in construction, operation, and maintenance.

THE WATER REUSE CONCEPT

There can be little doubt that the ultimate and logical solution to both the water supply and water pollution control problems, especially in the densely urbanized sections of the world, is recirculation of water, i.e., its complete treatment after use and its distribution again as potable water within the same or the downstream municipality.[28]

[28] The literature in this area is only beginning to emerge, and primarily it covers the technical aspects. Other types of analyses are also needed since complex regulatory and administrative considerations are involved, and positive civic leadership is often required.

A basic source is *Present and Prospective Means for Improved Reuse of Water* by the U.S. Senate (reference 104), which is a broad survey of the problem. A great number of discussions have appeared recently in the periodic literature, and it is impossible to list even a representative selection. Anybody interested in the subject would do well to look in the indices under the following place names: Lebanon, Ohio; Santee, California; Pomona, California; Lake Tahoe, California and Nevada; and Whittier Narrows, California, which are the locations where the more significant testing of the reuse concept in the United States is currently taking place (references 15, 21, 84, 85, 91, and

The current obstacles to a wider use of this concept are costs and psychological uneasiness. But both of these problems are bound to be minimized as present trends continue. It is safe to predict that the costs of water reuse will decrease absolutely as more efficient purification methods are developed and relatively as the readily available sources of drinking water become exhausted around all metropolitan areas, and fresh water has to be brought in at great expense from outlying locations.

The reluctance of the population to use "secondhand" water could be possibly overcome by pointing out two facts. First, there is ample practical and experimental evidence to show that wastewater can be reliably and continuously purified to any desired degree of cleanliness, and the general public today is conditioned to accept technical evidence. Second, practically everybody knows these days that the amount of water available to our planet remains constant; it only circulates continuously through the atmosphere, rain, water courses, soil, and seas back to the atmosphere. Consequently, we are always drinking water which has recirculated already thousands of times through evaporation which leaves all impurities behind and, more often than we would like, we are using recent discharges from an upstream community which have not been adequately purified, since they have not gone through the complete cycle, but are safe from the medical point of view.

The water reuse concept which has emerged as a dominant topic in the past few years in this country is thus nothing new, nor does it necessarily involve any new engineering methods beyond those discussed previously. It is rather an organizational and utility systems' coordination task.

---

129), or Chanute, Kansas, where water had to be recycled under emergency conditions even though its quality was inferior.

A few of the recent standard sanitary textbooks contain discussions of the subject (reference 16) and there are chapters in some reference works on water treatment (reference 84). A collection of papers from an ASCE conference on watershed development and control (reference 60) includes examinations of the use of wastewater for irrigation and ground water recharge, as well as general pollution problems. There are even suggestions as to how the regenerative closed-cycle idea can be applied to river basin management through the use of space technology (reference 23).

One of the first problems encountered here is the decision whether to recirculate the water within the boundaries of a single political unit or whether to look at a chain of communities, if they are close together, along a river as a linked watercourse system. To recirculate water within the same municipality entails an additional cost beyond that of the required treatment: pumping of the water from the lowest point back to the highest. But it can be organized under the same governmental administration utilizing funds from a single budget. A chain system is more efficient from the engineering point of view since gravity flow can be utilized to a large extent, but the administrative and management complications have been a consistent problem. Why should an upstream community spend its funds to assure good water supply for the lower one? Reorganization and modification of present administrative practices or participation by higher levels of government will be required, as discussed in Chapters 2 and 5.

Since the technical concept of water reuse is rather simple, but its execution may take a number of forms, the subject can best be investigated by several examples.

NEW PROVIDENCE, BAHAMAS. One such interesting case is New Providence Island, in the Bahamas, on which the City of Nassau is located. It is a place with a crucial water shortage since the only source is rain water that can be trapped on the land area. The island is beginning to face a sewage pollution problem because of intensified development. If a conventional approach were used, a definite ceiling would have to be placed on the growth of the city and island by the limited available water supply. This equals the total rainfall on the island minus losses through evaporation and seepage into the sea which restrict the total amount recoverable for municipal purposes.

To break this straitjacket, a desalting plant[29] has been built, and

[29] Desalting of sea water is often confused with reuse of wastewater. Obviously they are two totally different concepts, although both serve to increase the water supply of a locality. The first opens, so to say, a new and previously untapped source and makes it usable for a price; the other avoids the problem of finding a new source, also at a price. Parenthetically, it can be mentioned that the effluent from a regular secondary treatment plant is 35 times purer than sea water, in terms of foreign material carried. Since secondary treatment is usually required under any circumstances, the additional costs for tertiary treatment may be quite justifiable economically in cases of water shortage and as compared to the costs of desalinization.

an enlargement of its capacity is proposed; it has even been suggested that water be brought by tanker from other presently undeveloped islands. Yet, all the conditions and characteristics point toward a reuse approach as a more promising answer.

As proposed by a recent study,[30] a full-scale recirculation system can be constructed in the interior of the island which can provide a permanent solution utilizing a closed water cycle. Rainwater would then only serve to replenish losses through evaporation and seepage; in practice it is expected that the existing conventional well fields and desalting plant will also be retained.

The sequence of purification steps would be the following: regular domestic sewage will be collected by the network of pipes within the city, pumped over a ridge and via an interceptor sewer to a treatment plant. The plant would provide regular secondary treatment (activated sludge), but the effluent from it would be passed first through a filtration network within a sand layer of about 150 acres. The surface of this area can be used for light recreational activities, particularly because the sewage plant would be located adjacent to a large national park. The liquid collected from the sand filter would be pumped into a series of artificial lakes for further sedimentation and oxidation. These ponds could be used for fish farming and boating, possibly even swimming at the downstream end. Finally the effluent would be discharged in the existing Lake Killarney which would act as a reservoir directly and would also contribute seepage flow to the available ground water volume. The major problem here is the high volume of evaporation due to the climate, not the question of water purity.

LAKE TAHOE, CALIFORNIA. Lake Tahoe is one of the first instances in the United States where a full-scale tertiary treatment process has been put into operation. The reason again was a crisis situation. For several years, with the gain in popularity of this recreational area, the waters of the lake were increasingly polluted, thereby raising the specter of killing the major attraction of the area.

The lake, subject to gradual eutrophication, was in danger of

[30] P. L. Wiener and F. Ferguson, *The Development Plan of New Providence Island and the City of Nassau* (government of the Bahama Islands, 1968).

experiencing a speeding up in this natural process due to the 6,000,000 visitors annually. Incremental and separate expansion of existing plants could never catch up with the increase in sewage volume. The administrations of 2 states, 5 counties, and 64 other governmental agencies were involved, and they all agreed on a solution: a $40 million expenditure for a central disposal plant and 3 outfall pipes which will carry the effluent outside the basin across mountain passes.[31]

The plant treating sewage from many communities was constructed in Bijou, California, and is among the most advanced facilities in the country. Effluent from the standard primary and secondary stages[32] is first coagulated with alum and a polymeric flocculant and then filtered through a sand bed which allows flocculation during filtration. This liquid is further purified through granular activated carbon columns, primarily to adsorb detergent particles, and chlorination. The final effluent is of better quality than the drinking water of many cities and villages, as shown by continuous monitoring of the environment.

OTHER EXAMPLES OF REUSE. A pilot plant at Pomona, California, reclaims about 8 mgd (million gallons per day) which is used for recreation lakes, irrigation, and industry.[33] Settling basins, biological treatment, and chlorination are used in the plant. The water will be sold to industry and farms at 25 per cent of the price of fresh water, or one tenth of the cost of desalted sea water. This operation is the first step in a $20 million program for the Los Angeles basin, which eventually hopes to reclaim 100 mgd.

The United States Public Health Service has a pilot research plant in operation at Lebanon, Ohio, which is a purely experimental installation obtaining 75,000 gallons of pure water from the effluent generated by 7,000 residents.[34] The process is rather involved since it takes the discharge from a conventional treatment plant and passes it through a diatomaceous filter which removes practically all

[31] "Keeping Tahoe Alive," *Time Magazine,* August 12, 1966.
[32] "Cash and Credit for Clean Waters," *Chemical Week,* December 4, 1965.
[33] As reported in *Business Week,* March 4, 1967.
[34] *The Wall Street Journal,* December 9, 1965.

suspended solids, an activated carbon filter which catches the remaining organic contaminants including oils and insecticides, and finally through an electrodialysis tank which removes inorganic salts.

The work at Santee, California, was initiated because of necessity—extreme local water shortage. Plans have been prepared for a completely closed recycling system; at the present the operations are more modest in scope. The effluent from a treatment plant (85 per cent of organic matter removed) is poured into a 16-acre lake for aeration, then pumped to 6 filtration beds from where the seepage is collected in a trench and conducted to a chain of 5 progressively cleaner lakes. These are already used for boating and swimming with no observable reluctance by the local population. In the future, water from these lakes will be picked up by an underground network of pipes and sold to industry and agricultural users. The water discharged by them, in turn, will be collected in natural basins and pumped back into the system.

Operations of limited reuse scope, such as the selling of water to industry and farming, can be found at several other locations in the United States: Amarillo, Las Vegas, and elsewhere. Of greater interest is the proposed system for Nassau County on Long Island, New York, which contemplates the construction of deep injection wells for the treated secondary effluent. Several objectives would be accomplished thereby: recharge of the ground water table, which is the source of local drinking water, and creation of a fresh water barrier against salt water intrusion.

Finally, at a completely different scale, the recirculation concept can also be applied to individual buildings or activities. For example, a method has been developed in Canada for laundries which removes only dirt and returns the water hot and saturated with the original detergent.

Similar systems may also be perfected for regular household use where only minor additions of water may be required to compensate for evaporation and other losses. Furthermore, if the duplication of pipes becomes economically feasible, separate systems for drinking water, washing, and toilet flushing can be imagined. A number of such partial improvements are already in operation. The application of this concept would not be only in such obvious cases as completely isolated buildings; the fact that it could eliminate the expensive water distribution and sewage collection networks suggests its possible use in light-density urban areas.

Definite conclusions will only come in the future. In the meantime the door has been opened slightly so that we are not restricted completely by conventional methods of environmental control, but can start to ask basic questions as to the optimum features of a waste disposal system: Should water circulate within the building and solid wastes be collected for casting away; should all solid wastes be also discarded in sewers through garbage grinding; or, should there be a combination of both systems as they exist today?

SUGGESTED RESEARCH

Establishment of procedures for detailed local soils surveys with interpretive analyses.

Definition of guidelines with cost estimates relating various collection network configurations to the physical conditions of the site and to service requirements.

Definition of guidelines for the selection of types of sewage treatment plants with cost estimates in relation to physical conditions of the site, community size, and service requirements.

Examination, through case studies, of the effects that treatment plants have on neighboring uses and preparation of guidelines for their location in the future.

Definition of conditions under which tertiary processes are required and investigation of suitable types.

Investigation of the potential use of sludge as a marketable product.

Investigation of the water reuse concept within a complete cost-benefit accounting system; detailed examination of available cases.

Examination of the experience with package plants and development of procedures for their use, planning, and control.

Further development of small, self-contained liquid waste control and recirculation units; research on their potential use.

Investigation of new waste collection methods, including packaging and concentration, as related to on-site or community-wide treatment methods.

Study of the long-range effects of controlled dumping, such as in oceans or abandoned mines.

Research analyzing the potential benefits related to the transformation of wastes from one physical state to another.

5

ADMINISTRATIVE AND REGULATORY ASPECTS

It is apparent from the listing of the various treatment methods in the preceding chapter that we have the technical capability and knowledge to deal quite adequately with liquid wastes; yet we are confronted by dirty rivers and lakes, by polluted beaches, by soiled drinking water sources, and by foul harbors across the country.

The answer as to why these conditions exist is provided partially by our hesitancy to spend money, although it appears that the required economic means are present. But the real key to the problem is to be found almost certainly under the label of administration, which includes policy formulation, program development, and resource allocation. It has been suggested repeatedly that the principal difficulties in contemporary environmental control are: (1) the gap between our technical knowledge and our ability to use it; and (2) the fact that many agencies are becoming involved in the effort to preserve our environment, but that they operate outside a coordinated system.[1]

These deficiencies, more specifically, include uncertainty about standards, disagreement as to who should set and enforce them, lack of effective agencies responsible for river basins, where water quality control can be best achieved, similar duties vested in several levels

[1] See A. A. Atkisson, "Urban Ecology: The New Challenge," in the *Proceedings of the 4th AMA Congress on Environmental Health Problems*, New York City, April 24–26, 1967, pp. 128–37.

of government, splintered responsibilities among municipal departments, legal encouragement of small systems, and conflicts of interests among water users as well as misunderstanding on the part of the public of the problems and aims of pollution control.[2]

A not inconsiderable part of the task of water quality control is the formulation of an administrative and governmental structure through which environmental quality control can be achieved and which is also capable of marshaling financial resources or enforcing ordinances to do the job.[3]

The planners' greatest participation and responsibility in the waste control field can be expected in the area of public administration, policy formulation, and organization of governmental resources. This can be regarded as a liaison function between the technical specialists and the elected officials who must receive advice as to what actions to initiate that would secure the maximum benefit for the community. To do this job adequately, planners must, of course, have an understanding of the technical aspects, but their direct contribution in this area will most often take the form of suggestions, arranged by priority, within the entire framework of public needs. Furthermore, since all the major elements in waste management are subject to political decisions, information and education of the electorate is a vital part of the planners' task.

SETTING OF PURITY STANDARDS

Of all the topics discussed in this chapter, the question of environmental quality levels is among the most vague and uncertain. This is

---

[2] General sources relating to the various administrative considerations discussed in this chapter are references 1, 2, 17, 19, 36, 40, 46, 67, 88, and 122 in the bibliography. Particularly significant and appropriate is Chapter III, "Providing Urban Services: The Case of Water Supply and Pollution," in *Metropolitan America: Challenge to Federalism,* prepared by B. J. Frieden for the Advisory Commission on Intergovernmental Relations (reference 39).

[3] A recent study commission appointed by the Governor of the State of Maryland has concentrated its attention on institutional matters and administrative arrangements, basically recommending local control over land use and socioeconomic objectives and proposing that the State assume a direct and broad service role, in effect, creating a statewide sanitary district. See A. Heubeck, Jr., et al., "Program for Water-Pollution Control in Maryland," *Journal of the Sanitary Engineering Division—ASCE,* SA 2, April 1968, pp. 283–93.

due to several factors. To begin with, there is no agreement among the experts as to what specific standards should be maintained or even what degree of pollution under any given circumstances is harmful to human beings, fishlife, and aquatic plants. Furthermore, there is a continuing upgrading of expectations and requirements of cleanliness. So that even if a "level of tolerance" in pollution could be defined for today, it is bound to change tomorrow.

It is to be noted that the standards mentioned above and discussed in the rest of this chapter refer to the water itself, i.e., the actual quality of the environment as experienced by humans, animals, and plants. These levels are also called stream or ambient standards as distinguished from raw material or input standards, and effluent or discharge standards.

Three broad levels of environmental quality can be distinguished: (1) direct health hazard, which may take the forms of a threat of instantaneous death or a great probability of succumbing to disease; (2) economic loss, such as the disppearance of commercial fish or increased costs of treatment for potable or industrial water, which does not endanger human life under normal conditions; (3) nuisance, which may express itself as a psychological and esthetic discomfort to human beings but has no tangible costs associated with it.

HEALTH HAZARDS. Criteria of water quality to assure the first level of environmental sanitation—survival—is not too difficult to determine, since it is purely a medical problem. But also here the long-range effect of slightly polluted water on human health is not well understood, and thus it is usually ignored. The subtle influence that changed water temperature, turbidity, chemical composition, presence of nutrients or poisons may have on plants or fish is even less defined. There may even be evolutionary changes in biological species to adapt themselves to the changed conditions in a desperate struggle for survival.

In this connection, the work done by some biological investigators in checking pollution levels is of interest.[4] This takes the form of an inventory, by number and type, of various life forms in a body of

[4] "Lifesaver for Sick Streams," *Chemical Week*, January 23, 1965.

water at different locations and time periods. For example, the effect of a new pollution source can be gauged by enumerating the aquatic animals and plants in a unit volume of water before and after the start of operations. Such monitoring systems can keep a close check on the pollution characteristics of a stream or lake; they may also provide enough data to enable specialists in the future to establish precise standards relating pollutants to their effect on biota, and thus enable scientists to predict the impact of various potentially harmful discharges.

The more obvious threats to life and survival presented by pathogenic bacteria are not difficult to identify and remove through chlorination if adequate care is exercised. This, the most dangerous aspect of water pollution, is not a problem today; the less direct and less apparent perils are the real menaces.

The residents of the industrialized countries like to believe that they have moved out of the stage concerned with the problems of survival and only have to worry about economic and esthetic aspects. But there is some discouraging and frightening evidence that, if present trends in pollution are allowed to continue, survival may be threatened again. Most of the people living in the developing countries, of course, have always been in this critical phase and remain so even today

ECONOMIC LOSSES. The second level in water quality relates to economic considerations which can be quantified theoretically in a cost-benefit analysis, provided that precise relationships between the amount of various pollutants and their effect on the environment can be defined. These problems have already been touched upon earlier,[5] and an example at this point should suffice. If a factory releases per day a given volume of a certain chemical, this will have a measurable impact on the receiving river: decrease the value of marketable fish by amount X per year, increase the water purification costs downstream by amount Y, and require an additional expenditure of Z dollars for boat and other floating equipment maintenance. This will result in a total loss of A dollars to the community per year. Amount A represents also the damage created by the manufacturer for which he

[5] See page 17, Chapter 2.

should be held responsible. If the annual treatment costs to remove the chemical at the source are less than amount A, then such treatment would be advisable at the source; if not, then the polluter may find it more advantageous, under governmental supervision, to compensate those who are suffering an economic loss.

The problem with this theoretical approach, as mentioned before, is the difficulty of practical execution, i.e., the finding of exact costs, losses, and benefits, and the precise assignment of responsibility in a situation where many polluters are in operation. A few other important aspects, such as esthetic and recreational uses of water, tend to be ignored.

NUISANCE. This brings up the third consideration—the unpleasantness, offensiveness, or "insult of the environment." The conceptual argument that humans should not have to tolerate or be exposed to visual or olfactory nuisances is accepted in its general form by almost everybody. The problem is to define nuisance in practical terms. The approach that can be advocated is to classify each body of water as to its purpose and use, and set standards accordingly. This is a common, widely used procedure giving practical results.

Consequently, the economic investigation has little to do with the setting of standards: cost considerations do not require the establishment of any specific levels, but form, rather, a continuous moving analysis of relationships up and down the scale. The conclusion must be drawn that environmental standards cannot and should not be set on an economic basis. They should rather be established through the definition of what the nation and the locality consider a minimum acceptable situation in terms of health, enjoyment, and ecological balance. These water purity requirements could then be moved upward if economic analyses justify them, but never downward regardless of the results of any cost calculations.

For example, anything may be tolerated in a stream flowing through an industrial district not accessible to the public and flowing directly to a treatment plant. The same stream, if visible to and approachable by people, should not carry floating or large pieces of material or give off smells. A river flowing through a city and used as a harbor or for boating, but not swimming, need not necessarily be crystal clear, but it should not carry any visible particles, have unnatural color, give off smells, or kill all fishlife. A creek running through a residential section should present no dangers to swimmers or waders and should support a flourishing aquatic life, even though it may not be of the purest drinking quality.

RANGE OF STANDARDS. As can be observed, this path toward the establishment of standards is more qualitative than quantitative. Purity levels would be defined by actual measurements expressed in numbers only where absolute precision is possible or necessary. This methodology may also be regarded as an interim approach awaiting the results of further scientific research.

The relationships among pollution loads, standards, and natural purification capacity of the environment are illustrated in Fig. 6. Starting with the irreducible amount of natural impurities which are continuously added to and absorbed by rivers and lakes without difficulty, further continuous infusion of man-generated wastes will reach a state where the self-cleaning capacity of the environment is becoming overpowered. The danger zone corresponds to an amount of pollutants from which the river or lake can recover, but whose presence creates a detrimental, albeit temporary, situation. This range can also be equated directly with a range of basic purity standards—any additional continuous discharge of waste will cause progressively deteriorating conditions, i.e., the environment will be saturated by pollutants. It is to be noted that in this example the standards are to be regarded as rock bottom, since they only guard against entry into a fully septic situation. In many instances the decision makers may be well advised to shift the tolerance level considerably to the left to avoid even the risk of approaching full pollution and to maintain a water quality level as required for higher uses.

A further complication in the establishment of standards is the often vociferous and even emotional attitude taken by various interest groups toward water quality levels. This ranges from the conservationists' adamant statements that absolutely nothing should be dumped into the environment to the industrialists' equally insistent

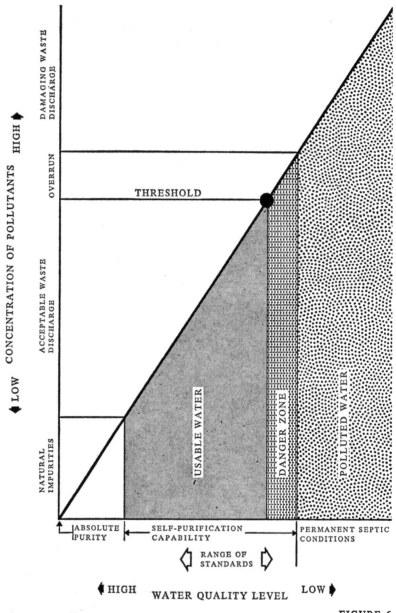

FIGURE 6

stand that the primary purpose of certain streams is to receive discarded wastes. A definition of purpose for each water course is the solution to this dilemma.

The writing of meaningful standards and criteria of water quality for any particular locality is thus not a matter of making blanket statements and finding guidelines from other municipalities. It requires first an understanding of the implications in economic, esthetic, and functional terms of the various proposed purity levels; second, it demands careful analysis and master planning of the water resources in the community.

We have, fortunately, moved away from the dominant practice of only a few years ago which simply stated in a general way that any discharges into a body of water should be at least as clean as the receiving waters. This practice, obviously, did not account for the cumulative effect of contaminants and offered no hope of ever cleaning up a polluted situation. The current attempt is not only to stop pollution increase but to roll it back. This attitude is also bolstered significantly by recent Federal legislation, notably The Water Quality Act of 1965 and The Clean Water Restoration Act of 1966. These acts established the requirement for setting water quality standards, increased authorization for Federal construction, research, and development funds, encouraged private business participation, and generally created a new approach toward the water pollution problem on a national scale.

EXAMPLES OF STANDARDS. The above discussion was not only a theoretical analysis; these concepts are now finding their practical manifestation in the difficult task that all states face in setting up specific water quality standards for various bodies of water. This is required by Federal agencies as a prerequisite to the allocation of financial aid for control works, and thus the generation of supreme interest in the subject is guaranteed.

A June 30, 1967, deadline was set for the states to submit their own standards to the Federal Water Pollution Control Administration (FWPCA) or else accept standards established by the Department of the Interior. To the surprise of many, almost all states met this deadline. While it is too early yet to evaluate them in a comprehensive way, a few characteristics can be observed as portents of the future approach in this field.[6]

Indiana's recommendations, which have been suggested as a model for others, include a minimum criterion for all waters at all places and at all times. They bar outright the following:

1. Substances attributable to municipal, industrial, and agricultural or other discharges that will settle to form putrescent or otherwise objectionable sludge deposits;
2. Flotating debris, oil, scum, and other floating materials in amount sufficient to be unsightly;
3. Discharges producing color, odor, or other conditions in such a degree as to create a nuisance;
4. Discharges in concentrations or combinations that are toxic or harmful to human, animal, plant, or aquatic life.

Because of the vagueness of several terms, many of these rules are subject to individual definition and open to deliberate misinterpretation. Administrative and enforcement problems, as well as court battles, can be expected. Yet, there is also good reason to believe that it will be possible to eliminate some of the more gross abuses of the water enviroment through the enforcement of these regulations and that a momentum may be established which will lead to improving conditions as standards become more precisely defined, penalties become stiffer, and the public at large recognizes and supports the attempts to restore quality to their living space. The pattern is, thus, becoming established wherein the states are given and have assumed the primary responsibility for determining stream standards accord-

[6] The approval procedure itself has, however, generated extensive controversy. For example, those states which have received full or partial approval of their standards by the Secretary of the Department of the Interior are upset by the announcement that reexamination with a view toward upgrading will be done periodically. Industries and municipalities have objected to the ruling that for streams whose present quality is higher than the standards no deterioration of purity is permissible, except under special but not well-defined conditions. On the other hand, conservationists would like to see much stricter requirements. Also, the old argument of Federal interference in state functions is raised; the orginal lack of concrete guidelines, prescribed timetables, sketchy research, and inadequate cost-benefit analysis have been attacked.

See *Chemical Week* of June 24, 1967, "The Rules Flow In," of December 30, 1967, "Water Rules: Slow Going," and of February 24, 1968, "Waging War on Dirty Water," and *Industrial Water Engineering* of February 1968, "A Plea for Reason in Pollution Control."

ing to the social and economic classification of their rivers and lakes.

A not very obvious but nevertheless important side benefit of the establishment of comparable nationwide water quality standards under Federal supervision may be the elimination of the old threat —moving to another state or community—that industries have been known to use when faced with resolute community demands to clean up their effluent. This factor has been one of the major reasons why state enforcement procedures have been notoriously deficient in the past.

The new statewide regulations are not the final word. Because of their comprehensive and overall character, it can be expected that much of the detailed quality determination and enforcement will come at the local level, where precise criteria can be established in line with particular conditions. It is to be hoped, however, that such ordinances can be set up or coordinated for whole regions or watersheds to assure balance within an ecological unit. The Ohio and Delaware River organizations, and a few others, are pointing the way; interstate pacts and cooperation across state lines will be necessary in several instances.

The set of quality standards established by the Delaware River Basin Commission is another example worth mentioning.[7] The basic principle of these regulations again is that water *use* shall be paramount in determining stream quality objectives which, in turn, fix effluent quality requirements. However, regardless of the specific objectives for each position of the river, all wastes shall receive a minimum of secondary treatment, which means the removal of practically all suspended solids and reduction of B.O.D. by at least 85 per cent, and all wastes containing human excreta are to be disinfected.

The New England Interstate Water Pollution Control Commission's standards are specified for four classes of streams based on the dominant use:

Class A water intended for general use, including human consumption after disinfection;

Class B water intended for recreation, bathing, and irrigation—

---

[7] *Civil Engineering*, June 1967.

good visual appearance, capable of supporting fishlife, and usable for public water supplies after filtration;

Class C water intended for boating, irrigation of crops which are cooked before eating, and industrial processes and cooling;

Class D water intended for liquid waste transport, power production, navigation, and some industrial uses.

The actual translation of all these descriptive standards into measurable physical and chemical maximum and minimum characteristics is still a somewhat uncertain procedure because the water environment is an extremely complex biological medium where secondary and tertiary effects in an interlinked system may be caused by various combinations of dissolved compounds and physical states. But experience and test results are gradually accumulating as a result of the continuous work of various scientists, and a precise listing (such as Appendix C) of the permissible ranges of specific pollutants for various purposes can be given. For example, taking only the dissolved oxygen levels as one criterion, we know that 10 parts per million (ppm) or milligrams per liter (mg/l) is ideal for the maintenance of fishlife, 5 ppm is an approximate threshold, and if the content drops below 3 ppm fish kills will result.

Reliance on such specific knowledge produces, for example, the rather simple stream standards of the State of Washington specifying that no wastes can be discharged which (1) will reduce the dissolved oxygen level below 5 ppm, (2) produce pH (acidity) measures outside the range of 6.5 to 8.5, and (3) generate toxic conditions of any kind.

ADMINISTRATION OF
WATER POLLUTION CONTROL

It is not the aim of this section to analyze and discuss the various forms of public and special agencies which can be and are used to provide community services. That is a subject which has been discussed from a number of points of view quite adequately;[8] the purpose here is

---

[8] See, for example, R. G. Smith, *Public Authorities, Special Districts and Local Government* (Washington, D.C.: National Association of Counties Re-

rather to review briefly some of the unique aspects of administrative and governmental organizations[9] arising from the special needs of liquid waste control.

Distinction has to be made at the very beginning between the two phases of public responsibility: control and regulation vs. actual operation of facilities. Although there appears to be a good amount of overlap, these two aspects can be separated; the emphasis in this section will be placed on the latter. The former has already been considered.

The basic question as to private vs. public ownership of utilities must first be considered. Occasionally suggestions are still made[10] that under certain conditions it would be advisable to delegate the responsibility for providing sanitary services to private companies through a utility franchise arrangement. In support of such proposals several reasons are advanced: first, that there has been a long history in the United States of private entrepreneurs supplying community services (ranging from garbage disposal to electric power) and that many city systems were originally thus constructed; second, that such action would free municipalities, as well as private developers, from the financial and administrative burdens of construction and maintenance of sewerage systems; and third, that private corporations can achieve better efficiency since they are unhampered by civil service slowdowns and can offer the advantages of large-scale operations even to small municipalities.

These arguments have to be rejected primarily because of the current and continuing development in attitudes toward essential public services. There is increasing acceptance of the concept that government should be completely responsible for those services that benefit the community as a whole, so that the control mechanism

---

search Foundation); R. C. Wood, *1400 Governments* (Cambridge, Mass.: Harvard University Press, 1961).

[9] An overall survey and description of these agencies is provided by Community Action Guide No. 4 in *Community Action Program for Water Pollution Control* (reference 88).

[10] E. J. Cleary, "Private Enterprise Prepared to Satisfy Sewage Disposal Needs," *Public Works*, July 1963 and August 1963, pp. 62–66 and 64–67, supports this possibility by citing the experience of such companies as Southern Gulf Utilities, Inc. and Suburbia Water and Sewage Systems which are equipped to provide any sanitary service, including the construction and operation of full sewerage systems.

utilizes democratic procedures, and the administration is directly accountable to the electorate who are the users of the system.

Furthermore, the specific arguments listed in favor of private operations can be countered rather easily. The history of private utility activity in the United States has shown continuously the dangers of abuse, non-concern with public interests, and graft under profit-motivated operations; the maintenance of a healthful environment is a governmental duty which cannot be delegated even if any one municipality has worked itself into a precarious financial situation; and small communities can benefit easily from large-scale operations if the entire control system is handled at a regional level.

It is interesting to note that private water supply companies were very popular and profitable in the United States up until the beginning of the twentieth century, since they could offer a crucially needed product for which the users were readily willing to pay. No such direct inducement existed with respect to sewerage since liquid waste disposal service could not be easily marketed: the waste generator saw no return in this, and, by simply not taking care of his own wastes, the individual could easily pass on these costs to the community by default.

The sanitary and community-structuring features of sewers cannot be left to private control. Most communities recognize this. The issue of private ownership was brought up primarily to apply the experience from the past to practices of today which have some similar characteristics: special purpose districts which are public operations but of a very localized scope. Most of the other public sewerage systems, with the exception of some Federal installations and a few metropolitan joint ventures, are constructed, maintained, and operated in the United States under the local municipal government directly.

SPECIAL DISTRICTS. Special districts, which have been created to operate a specific service and are largely financially independent, can be found today in all metropolitan areas immediately outside the central city and at numerous other locations within the United States serving small localities. The direct reasons for their emergence after World War II were the refusal by the administrators of the existing central systems to extend their service, such as sewer lines, very far into other political units, and the inability of the new suburban municipalities to finance a complete set of utilities. Thus they have been established usually in response to a purely localized problem on an ad hoc basis. Nor is this a unique problem in the United States; very similar organizations can be found in many other countries.

The difficulties created by the use of special districts in a pseudo-governmental capacity are well understood by now. The principal shortcomings are the problem of public control and the fragmentation of services that could be more efficiently provided on a larger scale. More specifically, this has resulted in numerous small systems offering inadequate treatment, duplicating facilities, and discharging effluent through a multitude of points. There are wide fluctuations in service levels and costs even between neighboring districts.

Yet, to say that new special districts should not be allowed to enter the sewerage field which should properly be the responsibility of general elected government, or that existing special districts should be speedily eliminated, would be an unrealistic and utopian wish under present circumstances. Regardless of the fact that this should be done in the long run, there are several reasons—all connected with present systems of public financing—that lead to the conclusion that special districts will be with us for some time, unless drastic reorganization of the local governmental systems are effectuated.

In the past, special districts had to be set up occasionally because municipalities lacked authority to provide certain types of service. These conditions have been removed today, and the present reasons for the existence of special districts are few.

One of them is the statutory debt limit of municipalities which can effectively stop new sewer construction if the borrowing capacity is about to be exhausted, as the recent experience in New York City has shown. The easiest way around this obstacle in smaller communities is to establish special districts which can float their own bonds and pay for them out of their own revenues. Since this is clearly a blatant effort to by-pass existing legislation, it may have to be used as an expedient, but is otherwise undefensible.

The other application of the special district concept can be found mostly in predominantly rural areas which are undergoing heavy subdivision activity and development. Under such circumstances, since the existing real estate improvements do not represent an adequate revenue base and the old residents are usually unwilling to "supply frills for the newcomers," even though sanitary services are needed, the special district device does make sense. However, as was pointed out previously, such organizations, their construction efforts, and the final improvements must be carefully controlled and fitted into a general plan. If these conditions are met, and guidance is exercised by a responsible public authority, special districts can be accepted as temporary operating agencies.

MUNICIPAL OPERATION. The preferred organization to provide sanitary services in the overwhelming number of cases is the local government (municipal or county) itself. That is particularly so from a theoretical public administration point of view, in light of the historical trend in this country which accepts more and more the premise that all those services which are needed by, or are useful to, the total citizenry should be offered and controlled by the public bodies responsible to the local electorate. The mistrust of local government generated during the last century, when corruption was common in public bodies, is also gradually being overcome. From a practical point of view, greater efficiencies can be achieved through operations on a larger scale, municipal revenues can be allocated according to overall needs, professionals can be engaged, and, most important, coordination among various utility services within the governmental structure is possible.

The real question that exists in this field today is to decide under what internal departmental arrangement can water quality control be best exercised. The traditional approach has been to set up a special and exclusive utility department for sewerage alone or for a combination of other public sanitary services (garbage, water). Coordination with other departments is essential to avoid potential duplication of such items as professional staffs and equipment. There is also the very fundamental problem that, if each waste—liquid, solid, and gaseous—is under the jurisdiction of a separate department, potentially efficient methods involving transformation from one physical state into another are almost impossible to consider, planning becomes very complex, and a high-level executive is missing.

The other conventional way of handling the problem is through a public works department which has responsibility for the construction and operation of all public facilities. In a large city, this may result in a tremendously complex organization with various branches that have little to do with each other except that they all utilize engineering skills and equipment.

A third type of organizational pattern—the grouping of activities by area of concern and final objectives—is gaining more favor at the present. Under this arrangement an environmental control or sanitary engineering department would be charged with the responsibility to maintain a defined quality level of urban livability, deal with all types of pollution, operate all the services, and be responsible for the enforcement of applicable ordinances. Such a department would not deal only with sewerage, but also air pollution, refuse disposal, street cleaning, and possibly water supply; and not only with engineering aspects, but also with policy, regulations, finance, and administration. This municipal housekeeping agency would be able thereby to work toward an integrated system of coordinated sanitary services which can be interlinked for maximum efficiency, as has been discussed at several points in this monograph. The recent efforts by Mayor Lindsay of New York City to reorganize the city's administrative structure are precisely in this direction and will warrant careful evaluation as experience accumulates.

REGIONWIDE ORGANIZATIONS. However, the intelligent use of local government procedures alone will not be able to overcome all the problems in the provision of sewerage services. It is not enough to say that most sanitary problems can be handled through the traditional and ubiquitous municipal agencies: public works, health, and utility departments. Because of the natural flow and dispersal of pollutants, and the efficiencies of large-scale operations, a geographically broad view has to be taken which does not fit easily into the standard governmental hierarchies. Political boundaries of a municipality or a county will only rarely correspond to the limits of a watershed—the logical unit for water-based utilities. There is even less likelihood that the problem areas of other wastes will coincide with these boundaries. However, reorganization on such a geographic basis will almost always be more desirable in terms of engineering efficiency, even if often political difficulties can be anticipated. But at least a strong plea has to be made for regional cooperation, conformity of standards within the watershed, and coordination of treatment activities.

It must be emphasized that the responsibility for pollution control will only occasionally fit within the state government, which has sometimes been suggested as the logical agency for this activity. The state may provide the enabling legislation for regional organizations and service authorities, it may enter into interstate compacts, it may do important work in research and system organization, and it may, most importantly, define stream standards, but it will not be quite suitable for the actual operation of pollution control works because of the nature of its responsibilities and the need to follow natural watershed boundaries.

The county government may be a more appropriate agency to assume responsibility for water pollution control works, but here too discrepancies between political and river basin limits are likely to exist. The advantages, however, are that an administrative mechanism already exists, provided that it is empowered to enter the sanitation field, and large-scale operations whose control is not exercised by a remote office are feasible and can be supported by the joint financial strength of many communities. In the several instances where such action has been undertaken,[11] the best results have been obtained through coordinated cooperative ventures between the county—which is responsible for the treatment facilities and interceptor lines—and the municipalities—which maintain and operate their own collection networks.

As a stop-gap and interim measure, contractual arrangements between administrative units can also be mentioned briefly. These are agreements to sell services across political boundaries in a purely commercial transaction. While such arrangements are much more common in water supply, they also exist in sewerage and other waste disposal. Central cities that have had, for example, excess capacity in their treatment plants have allowed suburban municipalities to discharge their sewage into the plant for a fee. In other cases, several

[11] See F. G. Goff, "Long-Range County Utility Planning," *Public Works,* September 1965, pp. 96–100, 134–35.

small municipalities have entered into a cooperative venture whereby one constructs and operates the plant, and the others participate in the financing.

Under no circumstances can contractual agreements be regarded as ultimate solutions, particularly because all the users of the system do not have control over operating decisions and the rate structure, but occasionally they may be a good step forward in achieving the semblance of a logical and large-scale system and can help municipalities which have exhausted their borrowing capacity.

Going beyond such arrangements, the familiar regional and metropolitan planning and intergovernmental coordination problems appear again, but with a few new features. Without entering into the matter very deeply, it can be postulated that, since a formal metropolitan government does not appear currently feasible but special-purpose cooperative actions hold greater promise, waste control is among the most obvious areas where such work could be fruitful. Very soon there may be no choice but to follow this path in a number of large cities.

There is also a question related to the scope of activities for a regional agency: Should it encompass many responsibilities under a single administration, thus allowing a comprehensive approach, or should each activity be housed in a separate regionwide agency with its own specialized staff, jurisdictional boundaries, and circumscribed scope of duties? The first alternative has a number of the earmarks of a regional government, thus it may be politically unacceptable and may be too vulnerable to attacks by all kinds of interest groups in various fields. In the water pollution control field, the second approach has emerged as the dominant one in the United States; such agencies may eventually absorb other functions as the political situation permits.

Of the several metropolitan areas whose experience in the coordination of sanitary control could be described here as examples,[12] Seattle offers a number of interesting features.[13] The decision makers

[12] Fort Worth, Miami, Kansas City, Phoenix, Pittsburgh, Detroit, Atlanta, Milwaukee, Washington, and Los Angeles.
[13] See "A City's Answer to Water Pollution," *U.S. News and World Report,* October 2, 1967, pp. 112–13, and "Seattle's Record-Breaking Sewage Treatment System," *Civil Engineering,* March 1965.

there considered several approaches to the improvement of service efficiency through large-scale operations and reached the pragmatic conclusion that a special purpose metropolitan agency appears to be the most realistic solution.

In the late 1950s the water quality in the numerous lakes, inlets, and bays of the region had deteriorated to intolerable levels, and it was obvious that waste treatment by each municipality was not only financially wasteful, but was insufficient to cope with the pollution problem under the best of circumstances. State enabling legislation was passed to allow metropolitan cooperation in sewage disposal, water supply, public transportation, parks, and a few other areas. The voters turned down this proposal at the first referendum, fearing that such a broad array of activities would swallow up their local independence.

However, after some efforts at public education and a reduction of the scope of the plan, the metropolitan agency was authorized soon thereafter to enter the water pollution control field and was backed with a $136 million bond issue. This, in turn, attracted state and Federal aids. A vigorous construction program of large treatment plants and interceptor sewers was initiated. Today the regional system extends over 290 square miles and takes care of 85 per cent of the sewage generated in the area, which consists of the City of Seattle and thirteen other municipalities.

Another example of metropolitan cooperation, illustrating particularly how sanitary services can be provided to the growing suburban belt within the present legal and administrative framework, is offered by the experience in the Minneapolis-St. Paul area.[14]

Legislation passed by the state empowered and charged the Minneapolis-St. Paul Sanitary District, which has been in operation since 1933, to prepare a detailed comprehensive plan for the extension of its lines into new territories and the enlargement of its treatment capacity. A joint committee guided the study project and determined the boundaries of the future service area in response not only to foreseeable land development but also recognizing the need to maintain

[14] G. E. Bodien, "Sewer Planning for a Metropolitan Area," *Public Works,* November 1964, pp. 87–90.

adequate water quality levels in several local rivers. The Metropolitan Planning Commission participated in the project by supplying the basic estimates of future conditions in the region. Sanitary engineering consultants and city engineers prepared the technical plans for the system.

Of particular interest is the plan for the fiscal structure, i.e., the apportionment of construction costs and future maintenance and operational expenses among the participating agencies. Trunk and interceptor sewer costs are allocated according to the maximum utilization rates expected in year 2000; treatment plant costs are distributed in a direct ratio to the average annual sewage volume from each subarea. It was also recognized that the presently sparsely developed suburban areas do not have enough financial strength to support large bond issues, and consequently it was proposed that the central cities finance part of the suburban facilities which would be repaid at progressively higher rates as the suburbs increase in population. These charges are to be made up of direct user fees based on sewage volume (50 per cent of total), a flat tax reflecting the increase in property values, and an acreage charge based on total developable land in each municipality which compensates for the need to build large sewers whose capacity will be greatly underutilized in the early years.

The other side of the coin in water quality control—the setting and enforcement of standards and general work in the prevention of pollution—has already been discussed, and only a few items need to be added here. One such point is that these regulations should have a hierarchical structure: general and broad policy established at the highest level (Federal), overall criteria defined at state level, and specific standards for actual areas and operational details formulated at the local level. We are on the way toward achieving this.

Another consideration is the overlap of jurisdictions and administrative responsibilities. Plans may have to be approved or reviewed by the local (city, town, or village) executive, legislative, health, and/or public works agencies, the county health department, state health department, and often also Federal agencies if grants or other financial aid from the national treasury are involved. Not infrequently there may also be extraterritorial jurisdiction on the part of other remote governmental units if watershed areas are involved. For example, the New York City Department of Water Supply exerts control over sanitary improvements in large parts of Westchester, Putnam, Sullivan, Ulster, Greene, and Delaware counties in New York State.

A closely related aspect of this complex regulatory structure is financial support. In the field of water pollution it is almost axiomatic that it is unreasonable and futile to impose control by a higher level of government without supplying some aid toward the achievement of the objectives of the corresponding agency. There are some encouraging developments in this field, and they will be discussed in a following section.

PUBLIC INFORMATION PROGRAMS

A democratic system can only operate and achieve objectives if the public understands and supports the community's goals. There are several elements involved here: reaching a consensus on the goals themselves, establishing the organizations and agencies which would carry out such policies (including the election of officials pledged to particular programs), and finding the means to effectuate the required improvements with public support. The last item is particularly important in the water pollution control field since almost invariably large expenditures are involved that require bond issues which, in turn, means that the local citizens have to approve a new financial burden for themselves.

Most of the actual efforts of any locality facing this problem have been devoted to the immediate and direct problem of securing a favorable referendum for a bond issue, i.e., selling the advantages of a completed plan.[15] The best results, however, have been obtained where the public has been involved from the very beginning: starting with the establishment of goals, not only at a point where specific amounts of money have to be found.

There would be little advantage in reviewing here all the approaches

[15] The available instructional literature is devoted mostly to the same problem.

that can or have been used in public information work since the procedures are largely the same for all public programs, and the issues and methods have been discussed repeatedly in professional publications.[16] However, there are a few unique aspects to sewage and water pollution control which have to be touched upon. First, the explanation of the work involves a number of terms and concepts which in a Victorian age would be considered unmentionable. Even today, a certain amount of delicacy may be required, although there is no reason why the proper precise technical terminology cannot be employed.

Furthermore, diplomacy is required in pointing out past mistakes in sanitary control as a reason for doing something better today. In addition to the usual problems involved here, this can appear to the local population as an accusation of dirtiness and slovenliness. Very few people will accept graciously the implication that they are negligent with their personal wastes when they take such care to use the latest deodorant. Obviously, tact is usually the advisable policy; occasionally there may be some beneficial shock value in a graphic explanation of the problem.

What makes the job of public information much easier these days than, let us say, three years ago is the appearance of a veritable flood or material in books, magazines, and newspapers which point out the seriousness of the pollution problem and document it rather well with actual experiences and cases. These works[17] do not present any new knowledge to the technician; they serve a more important purpose: making the general public aware of the impending disaster. And while they are primarily reportages, they also supply a wealth of illustrative examples which can illuminate many facets and characteristics of the environmental quality problem. They are written for the layman, and, because the subject affects everyone, these publications provide absorbing reading material in the tradition, although not always of the quality, of Rachel Carson's *Silent Spring*.

[16] A first-rate primer is contained in the aforementioned *Community Action Program for Water Pollution Control*, "Guide No. 8, Gaining and Maintaining Public Acceptance for Pollution Control Programs" (reference 88).

[17] See references 9, 13, 20, 38, 45, 47, 54, 76, 94, 115, and 116 in the bibliography. It should be noted, however, that no effort was made to list there even the major articles in the periodic press; the full-size books alone constitute a respectable library.

DRAFTING OF ORDINANCES

The task of writing regulations and ordinances in the sanitary field is a complex undertaking, primarily because of the uncertainty of standards and the best methods of achieving them if they are defined. Clearly the legal profession enters here beside the engineering, public health, administrative, and planning disciplines, and the work must be guided within the context of all applicable local, state, and Federal regulations in force at any one time. Several types of ordinances, regulations, and laws have to be distinguished within this broad area.

If we leave aside for the moment various Federal requirements, the first of these is state enabling legislation giving authority to municipal governments or special purpose agencies to enter the water pollution control field. Usually these laws involve grants of power to construct sewer networks and treatment plants, to issue bonds for that purpose, to collect fees, and to accept Federal grants and other forms of aid. Generally speaking, this type of legislation has been enacted across the United States, but there may be a necessity for modifications and amendments for any one state to reorganize administrative structures, to broaden sanitary responsibilities, and to improve budgetary operations. While all this is primarily a legal and legislative problem,[18] the determination of general objectives as a basis for state laws is a task which involves also the technical professions. Much work remains to be done at the state level to permit and encourage joint regional operations.

The other type of control that states customarily, although not always, exercise over water pollution is through direct quality regulations. A separate state agency may be established or an existing one empowered to deal with the problem. A master plan for the social and economic use of the water courses within the state should be prepared and would consist principally of a classification of all rivers and lakes according to their intended use[19] with defined permissible levels of waste discharges

---

[18] See USPHS, *Recommended State Legislation and Regulations* (reference 137), which offers drafts of suggested state enabling and control legislation.
[19] This work has been described also in the section devoted to Purity Standards.

All this, of course, has to be accompanied by proper public notices and hearings before final enactment. Violations can thus be treated as public nuisances and prosecuted accordingly. The effectiveness of the procedure depends on the quality of monitoring systems and enforcement, as well as the ability of present and potential polluters to pay for the required treatment facilities. The record so far has not been spectacularly bright.

The bulk of the pollution control work, however, will have to be accomplished at the local level where the needed detailed supervision can be exercised. Several types of municipal regulations can be used to achieve the objectives, and there is considerable overlap among them, thus requiring careful coordination to avoid conflicts. The aims of these ordinances are to control the use of municipal sewer systems and define permissible discharges, to supervise the construction and operation of private disposal facilities, and to assure that development of the city proceeds within the limitations established by utility services or site conditions.

A number of ordinances can be used to achieve these objectives, and they are listed below separately with an indication of their purpose, scope, and enforcement agency.

The zoning ordinance of the city is of paramount significance in regulating the private development so that it will not place any excessive or unforeseen loads on sanitary facilities. It is the main tool available to protect private properties from harmful actions by the owners themselves and their neighbors and generally to achieve a livable and sanitary environment.

Subdivision regulations is the second similar means of control. It applies primarily only to suburban areas undergoing development, but these are districts in particular need of quality control. Subdivision regulations can and should establish the requirements for construction of sewage collection lines, their connection to community systems, or, if this is not possible, provide for the establishment of special districts and private small-scale systems or, if this too is not feasible, allow septic tanks under strict supervision and control. The clauses of the so-called capped sewer ordinance, which require the construction of a sealed-off collection network in anticipation of a future public system, can be incorporated in subdivision regulations.

A comprehensive sanitary code for the municipality is another powerful tool in the inventory of local regulations, since it can deal with general standards, methods of sewage disposal, control of individual systems, and many other aspects of water pollution and quality protection. It is primarily an ordinance based on health considerations and thus properly under the jurisdiction of the health department. But since many of its clauses have great impact on the community and its operations, the preparation of this code should be coordinated with the work of the planning department to achieve overall municipal objectives. Planners will certainly have to be intimately familiar with its provisions.

If a sewer system exists in the city, its use will usually be regulated by a separate ordinance,[20] primarily specifying what type and character of discharges may be released from private properties into the network. This ordinance has to be under the direct control of the department operating the sewer system and will be largely technical in nature. Coordination with other agencies is required in the initial definition of quality levels according to the overall municipal environmental policy. The clauses of the ordinance may be very specific and permissible emission characteristics can be precisely defined, or they can be left rather general in nature—giving discretionary powers to the enforcement officer (sanitary engineer or public works expert).[21]

SUGGESTED RESEARCH

Further analysis of all levels of government as to their role and potential strengths in pollution control work.

---

[20] The Department of Health of the State of New York has published acceptable standards, procedures, and plan formats for major waste treatment works as well as individual household systems (reference 111). Construction codes and specifications are also included in the various manuals of ASCE-WPCF and FHA (references 65, 66, and 35).

[21] A complete proposed ordinance on sewers can be found in WPCF Manual No. 3 (reference 117) which supplies explanations of each clause allowing a municipality to regulate the construction and use of sewer systems by individual property owners. Some other general manuals (references 88 and 133) contain suggestions toward the drafting of ordinances also.

Investigation of the feasibility of control agencies at the river basin level.

Examination, with case studies, of special district performances in waste control.

Analysis of the dilution and self-purifying capacity of the water environment under a range of conditions.

Definition of methods for the determination of water quality standards under various conditions (levels of tolerance under specific conditions for specific purposes).

Examination of the importance of functional and economic aspects in pollution control vs. esthetic and other social considerations.

Establishment of a comprehensive record-keeping system of data related to pollution for local communities and regions.

Establishment of a coordinated mapping program for all utilities serving a given area.

Investigation of the most effective and productive public education and information procedures.

Preparation of complete standard ordinances or portions thereof related to waste control.

6

FINANCIAL ASPECTS

There is no question that in order to achieve any respectable environmental quality level in an urban situation considerable expenditures are involved. Even under the most progressive resource recycling program, only a small fraction of the costs can be recovered. The basic task is one of removing obnoxious or harmful elements from the water medium, an action which by itself does not create any new positive values but only removes artificially created negative conditions.

However, it has to be stated that if a society really wants a clean environment, and this objective is placed high enough on its list of priorities, any degree of purity is technologically possible. The ultimate decision rests with the community and, particularly within the industrialized countries, it will get what it is willing to pay for out of the total funds available for public expenditures and improvements.

The evidence of current city residents' response and pressure indicates that the public at large has recognized the importance of clean air, water, and soil, has become concerned, and is willing to spend money for it. The voters of New York State approved a $1.7 billion bond issue in 1965 for pollution control; other state and local programs have received broad-based support. And it is well to remember that the costs can be reduced if regional facilities are constructed, i.e., economies of scale are exploited. The analysis of actual construction expenditures indicates that, for example, costs for a secondary treatment plant serving a 100,000 population will be 5 to 7 times lower on a per capita basis than a plant for a service area of only 1,000 people.[1]

The specific costs to each producer of wastes or a municipality providing control services will include any or all of the following items:[2]

a. Production process changes, or changes in waste disposal methods for households.
b. Waste collection and transport facilities (capital costs plus operation and maintenance).
c. Treatment facilities (capital costs plus operation and maintenance).
d. Purchase of land for physical facilities.
e. Construction and operation of monitoring systems, including performance checking.
f. Work on receiving bodies of water to improve their absorption capacity.
g. Overall administrative expenses, including those of policy determinations and public relations.
h. Effluent charges, if any, imposed by other authorities; liability for damages.

For a waste management organization to achieve a given level of environmental quality, its capital and operational costs will be a function of the following:

a. The amount and type of wastes generated.
b. The topographic and hydrological features of the area.
c. The spatial distribution of the generation points.
d. The available methods of handling and disposal.
e. The political and local attitude toward the need for waste control.

The dimensions of the problem are indicated by several recent estimates attempting to determine the financial investment that would be required in water pollution control works within the foreseeable

---

[1] See Appendix D.
[2] See reference 145.

TOTAL CONSTRUCTION REQUIREMENTS

FOR SEWERAGE WORKS IN THE

UNITED STATES, 1967 TO 1980

(IN BILLIONS OF 1966 DOLLARS)

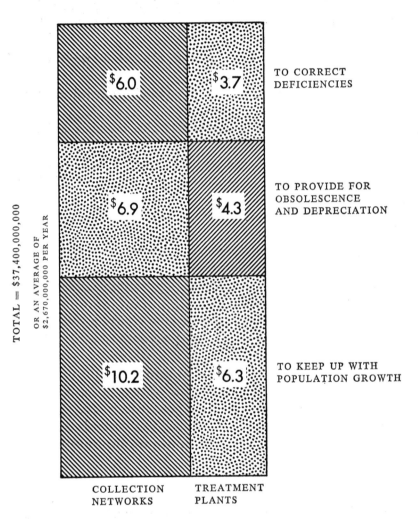

(LAND COSTS & MAINTENANCE NOT INCLUDED)

SOURCE: BUSINESS AND DEFENSE SERVICES ADMINISTRATION,
U.S. DEPARTMENT OF COMMERCE

FIGURE 7

future. Since about one quarter of all municipalities dump completely untreated wastes in the nation's rivers and lakes and another 30 per cent provide only primary treatment (1966), the total bill for needed treatment facilities up to the year 2000 would amount to $100 or $110 billion, approximately one year's national budget.[3] The U.S. Public Health Service has estimated that at least $700 million should be spent annually during the next decade simply to catch up. In the meantime, population and pollution continue to grow and, if nothing is done, wastes from 85 million people will have to be discharged raw in streams and lakes.

The Federal Water Pollution Control Administration believes that $26 to $29 billion should be spent over the next five years to construct collection and treatment facilities for municipal wastes. Industry will have to budget $3 to $5 billion to build new water treatment plants or upgrade existing ones within the next five years to meet new water quality standards.

Another study by the Business and Defense Services Administration[4] places the total needed expenditures, excluding company owned industrial waste water facilities, at $37.4 billion over the next fourteen years. As shown in Figs. 7 and 8, this amount of new investment would remove present deficiencies by 1980, rebuild obsolete plants, and keep additional construction in pace with the population increase. This is what should be spent in the technologically most advanced nation. Will it be?

The one general estimate that is accepted by most investigators is that pollution control expenditures will have to double in the next ten years, compared to present U.S. outlay. The other side of the coin is, of course, the fact that industries supplying equipment and materials are facing a growth situation. The chemical industry, for example, which at the present time sells $350 million worth of chemicals per year to water purification and waste treatment plants

[3] As reported in *The New York Times,* December 21, 1965. These, as well as the other figures in the following few paragraphs, can only be regarded as rough approximations since investigations have been made with differing assumptions and criteria. Yet, they fall within a range, and are used here only for illustrative purposes. See also E. P. Partridge, "The Costs of Control," *Industrial Water Engineering,* February 1968, pp. 16–20.

[4] K. L. Kollar and A. F. Volonte, *Regional Construction Requirements for Water and Wastewater Facilities, 1955–1967–1980* (reference 75).

SEWERAGE WORKS CONSTRUCTION LEVELS
IN THE UNITED STATES, 1955 TO 1980

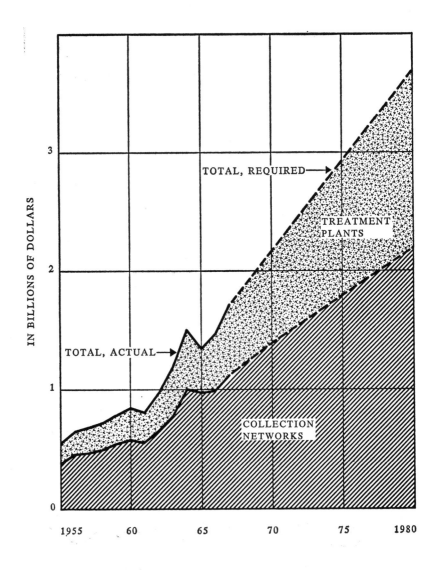

SOURCE: BUSINESS AND DEFENSE SERVICES ADMINISTRATION,
U.S. DEPARTMENT OF COMMERCE

FIGURE 8

can expect to increase their business to $650 million at the end of ten years.

Current actual expenditures, which have been estimated at about $600 to $900 million per year by municipalities for treatment facilities and $125 million per year by industry,[5] are not even enough to assure that the over 5,000 communities and 33 million people in the United States in need of improved facilities will be helped substantially. But there is room for some optimism if the cutback in domestic expenditures during the last two years, traceable to the Vietnam war,[6] can be regarded only as a temporary disturbance in the increasing amounts and rates of investment in pollution control facilities, and if the current entangled procedures can be regarded only as growing pains.

Federal financial aid ever since the Depression has been a major source of funds for the construction of local facilities, and it has also prompted and induced higher state and local expenditures through its matching grants requirements. Particularly active periods have been the 1930s, late 1950s, and early 1960s.

Within the last decade the Federal government has provided $865 million as its share in spurring a total construction in waste control works of about $4 billion serving 60 million people.

FEDERAL AND STATE PARTICIPATION

A number of Federal and state programs have been established in response to the recognized environmental pollution problems, and they have served to establish a foundation for further action through their modest accomplishments.

[5] "Dirty Water: Government Eyes Tax on Cities, Businesses That Pollute Streams," *The Wall Street Journal*, April 15, 1965. Other investigators estimate that industry spends now $400 million per year, but admit that the figure should be over $1 billion per year: "Billions to Clean Up the Rivers," *Business Week*, April 24, 1965, pp. 50–58; "Close at Hand: Tough Water Bill," *Chemical Week*, September 25, 1965, p. 30; "Cleaner Water Drive Steps Up," *Business Week*, March 13, 1965, pp. 78–80; "Pollution Fight Picks Up Force," *Business Week*, November 13, 1965, pp. 109–17.

[6] "War Spending May Curtail Big Water Projects and Pollution Abatement," *Engineering News-Record*, January 26, 1967, pp. 112–14.

Since these programs[7] are modified frequently, the state programs vary from place to place, and the allocated funds can be exhausted rapidly, any catalogue of such governmental aids becomes soon outdated. Even so, while no attempt will be made to include here an inventory of state programs, the list below of Federal programs may serve as a guide to the current (early 1968) conditions and as an illustration of U.S. government concern:

A. *Water and Sewer Facilities Grants*

Grants of up to 50 per cent of costs of land and construction of new facilities for a local public body, if there is an official areawide program and a comprehensive plan. (Housing and Urban Development Act of 1965.)

B. *Grants and Loans for Public Works and Development Facilities*

Grants of up to 50 per cent of development costs for various public facilities including sewer systems for jurisdictions designated as redevelopment areas (with high unemployment or low income). In severely depressed areas, up to 80 per cent Federal contribution is allowed. Loans for the full cost are also available. (Public Works and Economic Development Act of 1965.)

C. *Water Pollution Control*

1. Grants for Comprehensive Basin Planning:
   to assist state and interstate agencies.

2. Research, Development, and Demonstration Grants and Contracts:
   to develop new and improved methods in water pollution control (up to 70 or 75 per cent of project costs).

3. Training Grants, Contracts, and Research Fellowships:
   to assist public and private non-profit agencies, institutions, and individuals.

4. Waste Treatment Works Construction Grants:

[7] See *Catalog of Federal Assistance Programs,* June 1, 1967, Office of Economic Opportunity, Executive Office of the President, which lists all the available programs, their nature and purpose as well as eligibility criteria; the brochure *Grants-in-Aid and Other Financial Assistance Programs* listing programs administered by the U.S. Dept. of Health, Education and Welfare (1966) and giving the present status of these programs; "New Federal Aid for Public Works," *Public Works,* May 1966, pp. 88–91. A brief historical review of these programs and their changes can be found in *Metropolitan America,* pp. 52 ff. (reference 39).

to accelerate local waste treatment works construction by public bodies. The grant may be 40 per cent, if the state contributes at least 30 per cent; and 50 per cent, if the state contributes 25 per cent. An additional 10 per cent is allowed for metropolitan areas if there is a comprehensive plan. The project must conform with enforceable water quality standards.

(Federal Water Pollution Control Act, as amended.)

In addition, the Federal government has direct responsibility for inland navigation, flood control, irrigation, power plant sites, national parks, and multipurpose river development, all of which can be linked to water standards and pollution control. Specific and concrete jurisdiction is exercised by United States agencies over navigable waterways and their water quality through various enforcement procedures, but these are not tied directly to financial aid programs.

A state governor or the Secretary of the Interior can initiate action through the Federal Water Pollution Control Administration to abate conditions in any polluted waterway. After research and documentation of the situation, a conference of all involved parties is called to analyze the problem and to agree upon corrective action. If this does not bring results, a public hearing will be held before a board appointed by the Secretary of the Interior. As a last step, Federal court action may be taken.

Up to the present time only one case, out of less than forty, has gone this far. Criticisms have been levied against this program because of the long, drawn-out procedures and the apparent lack of vigor in the enforcement actions.

Several other Federal programs and regulations concerned with less direct aspects of general water quality incorporate financial assistance. They include such considerations as release of water from reservoirs to improve water quality during low-flow periods, water resources planning grants to local and state agencies, assistance to Indians and Alaskan natives for the construction and maintenance of sanitary facilities, special supplementary grants to severely depressed areas (such as Appalachia) and for planned metropolitan development (under the Demonstration Cities and Metropolitan Development Act of 1966).

One of the most important areas of Federal contribution to a better water environment is in research. A number of U.S. agencies are engaged in theoretical studies and experimentation, largely related to public health; these findings become available to the public at large.[8] Significant results and improvements in methods and equipment have been achieved by this work benefiting local communities in a practical way and advancing the entire field of sanitation.

Finally, the general planning assistance programs, which reach into numerous large and small communities across the country, provide funds to analyze local sanitary problems within the context of master plan studies. The aggregate contribution of these projects in the sanitary field is quite considerable, even though they suffer from a purely local approach and are not usually distinguished by penetrating investigations in those chapters of the reports devoted to pollution control.

It is not to be assumed, however, that these programs can solve the entire problem. The Federal government obviously could not do it alone, even if it assumed environmental control as one of its primary responsibilities and initiated a program comparable in scope to the series of highway construction projects. The present approach has to be regarded as a temporary or pump-priming activity before the entire pollution control problem and its financing can be placed on a rational basis. Regardless of the home rule and state rights implications, which are serious enough by themselves, there are two aspects which speak against a completely centralized national control.

The first of these is the already discussed question of standards. A basic national standard is needed to establish minima applicable to all sections of the country satisfying basic human, biological, and productive requirements. To achieve this level, Federal aid out of national revenues would appear entirely appropriate, especially for those sections of the country that at present are not able to carry these costs themselves.

Yet, every state or region, but not necessarily each small municipality, should have the right to improve upon the minimal standards

---

[8] For a complete listing of these efforts see L. W. Weinberger, "Government Research Trends," a paper presented during the Conference on Water Pollution held March 16–17, 1967, at Princeton University, N.J.

and to enforce such control. Enforcement carries with it financial responsibility again, and many states have gone beyond their traditional tasks in pollution control: provision of administrative and financial tools for local governments, enforcement of public health regulations, and concern with recreation and conservation. A half of all the states have established water pollution control boards, and a number of them[9] have lately organized financial aid programs for local sewerage works.

The only long-range approach that can be suggested in pollution control, regardless of the mechanics of achieving it, is to adopt the concept that the removal and destruction of wastes is a part of the production process which originated them in the first place. In other words, if somebody manufactures and sells a refrigerator he should be responsible for its ultimate destruction and harmless disposal. If somebody manufactures, let us say, detergent which creates liquid waste by-products, it is his responsibility to prevent such materials from affecting adversely other members of the community. Even more, he should also be made responsible for the ultimate disposal of the product itself after its useful life, particularly if there is a possibility that the final wastes may place excessive loads on existing treatment facilities. Needless to say, these costs will be passed on to the consumer, but there would be at least a built-in economic leverage assuring that products which create significant pollution problems would carry a premium cost, thereby contributing funds for treatment, and that the manufacturer would have to be legally answerable for his product's effect on the environment. This is nothing more than the responsibility now expected from drug manufacturers who are involved only a little more directly with human health and welfare.

This then is the second reason why governmental aid programs should not be regarded as a final means toward a solution—not that they are unsatisfactory per se, but rather that they are generally established in response to crisis situations, and that the responsibility for the removal of wastes should rest with its producers. This does not by any means preclude governmental financial participation and

[9] Maine, Maryland, New Hampshire, New Mexico, New York, Oregon, Pennsylvania, Vermont, and others.

help which will be sorely needed for a long time to come. Each municipality should certainly have the right to remit the disposal charges for individual manufacturers if it finds it advisable, but a directly linked cause-and-effect system appears to be a logical basis. This concept can be advocated, even recognizing the formidable practical difficulties of administration and enforcement, which appear to involve complicated bookkeeping. This problem, however, can be assigned to electronic computers.

Finally there is practical evidence that our current fiscal aid programs are far from being successful. To begin with, the funds are inadequate and not always appropriately distributed. There are also indications that the construction of pollution control works has even been retarded recently because of the Federal largesse which promises funds but does not always have them available for all who could use them. It takes a really courageous mayor to put the already strained municipal credit on the line when there is some chance that the Federal government may be forced to make a contribution if things get very bad.

LOCAL MEANS

Returning to the conventional methods of financing pollution control outside Federal and state aids, several local sources of funds can be considered.

These are (a) general obligation bonds coming under the municipal debt limit restrictions; (b) revenue bonds which are outside debt limits but carry higher interest rates and require the collection of user charges; and (c) special assessments against property owners who would benefit from the improvements.

Municipal bonds, by far the most important source of funds, have been discussed in numerous publications over the years.[10] The problems here, related to enabling legislation, municipal debt limits, credit rating, types of bonds, and fiscal management,[11] are the same

[10] For example, "Community Action Guide No. 6," in *Community Action Program for Water Pollution Control* (reference 88).

[11] New York City had been ordered (as far back as 1949) by the Interstate Commerce Commission to place in operation 17 treatment plants by 1959 to cope with its 1.3 billion gpd discharge. The Korean War with its building

as for most other capital improvements and require no further elaboration.

The urgency of the situation has resulted in interesting modifications of the traditional financing procedures: the exclusion of new sewage facilities from the debt limit, and cooperative efforts among separate jurisdictions to achieve a more efficient system. The latter actions are particularly significant since they prove the feasibility of extensive regional arrangements. In most of these instances, a contractual agreement is reached between the various jurisdictions whereby a treatment facility is operated by one municipality accepting, for an agreed upon compensation, the sewage from others.[12] Beyond technical economies due to large-scale operation, there are also savings in administration costs and, most important, a possibility is offered to structure a liquid waste control system according to intrinsic needs and physical determinants, not political boundaries.

Lastly, pay-as-you-go financing may also be considered as a method in sewer construction. However, it is not widely used because the expenditures are usually large, and the accumulation of such sums of money under an inflationary situation is rarely feasible or wise.

Unique approaches have been developed to obtain revenues for the repayment of borrowed funds. There are several means available, including general areawide taxes with revenues credited toward the amortization of a bond issue, or taxes on a special district basis, thus by-passing the debt limits of municipalities. In addition, service charges may be collected directly from the users of the utility, usually in some relationship to the actual use by individual customers. This measure may be the amount of water consumed or sewage meters may be installed for heavy producers of effluent, and rates may even be adjusted according to the strength of the sewage. On the other

---

material shortages intervened, and in 1957 the deadline was extended to 1967. Construction has still lagged badly, caused largely by insufficient construction funds and the exhaustion of the municipal borrowing capacity; the year 1967 has passed without the city being able even to approach the completion of the program. Further progress is greatly jeopardized by recent cut-backs in Federal funds available as construction grants. These appropriations are now at less than one-third of the authorized level.

[12] Some of these can be found in Seattle, Wash., Washington, D.C., Chicago, Ill., Boston, Mass., and Hartford, Conn.

hand, flat rates may be applied, regardless of the actual flow, but classified by types of users.

Finally, a change in traditional attitudes can also be observed in the emerging cooperative efforts between private industry and local government. This has been fostered by the growing pressure from communities compelling industry to embark on a more active construction program of liquid waste control works and, on the part of industry, the recognition that such demands will be enforced and the discovery that higher levels of government are willing to participate in the financing of facilities. The problem with respect to the last aspect is, however, that such public aid is intended for regular domestic sewage systems and not heavy industrial discharges. However, if joint municipal-industrial action is undertaken, in practice it becomes difficult to separate out the factory wastes.

As has been shown in a number of places,[13] cooperation through the sharing of construction costs is entirely feasible and beneficial for everybody concerned. Even if a few manufacturing plants receive a minor subsidy in the process, not much opposition can be generated to this since the public is the gainer, after all, through the improvement of water quality.

The advantages to the manufacturers, beside the easing of the financial burden, are obvious: operational unit costs are lower because of larger scale facilities and dilution with domestic wastes, and the public agencies usually assume the responsibility for plant site acquisition, which can be a serious problem in high-value industrial districts. In turn, large companies can often advance funds at crucial stages unencumbered by tedious governmental procedures. Some of the help that industry would like to have more widely available, in addition to direct sharing in governmental grants, are tax credits or rapid tax write-offs for pollution control equipment.[14]

Finally, as a long-range future possibility in the financing and

[13] In Davis, Calif. (Hunt's Foods), Lawrenceburg, Ky. (Kraft Foods), Monsanto, Ill. (Monsanto Co.), South Charleston, W. Va. (Union Carbide), Huntington, W. Va. (International Nickel) and others. See "Partnerships Cut Pollution Tabs," *Chemical Week,* February 5, 1966.

[14] Industrial waste tax benefits are currently in effect in Connecticut, Georgia, Idaho, Maine, Massachusetts, Michigan, New Hampshire, New York, North Carolina, Ohio, Rhode Island, South Carolina, Vermont, Virginia, and Wisconsin.

administration of water pollution control, instead of continuing to regard this work as a municipal service, it could be reorganized as a regionwide public utility. A large, government-controlled agency could conceivably achieve many of the efficiencies discussed previously under the comprehensive watershed structure regarding all polluters, private or public, as equal participants. In concept, such operations have already started at several locations in the form of regional agencies. The difference is that the existing operations are not a direct and integral part of governmental responsibilities, otherwise their functions are largely the same, including regulatory and revenue-generating powers.

SUGGESTED RESEARCH

Continuous inventory and evaluation of all applicable state and Federal programs in any one locality.

Further investigations in the correlation of construction and operational costs of sewage control works to basic community parameters.

Examination of methods for cost allocations among waste generators.

Exploration of the effectiveness of various inducements to achieve environmental control.

Study of the advantages and disadvantages of effluent charges.

Analyses of all waste management costs under varying administrative, regulatory, physical, and political conditions.

Survey of conditions that would encourage reuse of materials and water.

Investigation of the proper scale for waste control works and systems to achieve optimum return on investment.

7

~~~~~~

LOCAL PLANNING
ASPECTS

The entire problem of water quality control appears quite different when regarded from the local point of view rather than from the regional as has been done in an earlier chapter prior to a discussion of the technical features. The preceding analysis, therefore, should serve as fundamental background information for the following examination of the implications of water quality control on city development and structure. These are aspects of supreme interest to the urban planner and other non-technical professionals and decision makers involved in the guidance of the growth and formation of specific communities. This approach is not simply a worm's eye view, trying to make the best of restrictions imposed from above. A number of specific considerations can only be solved at the local level, and major policy decisions made with respect to the entire watershed may not be compatible with the objectives of each and every small town and village in the area. Furthermore, the actual effects of planning and development control work can be observed first, of course, on parcels of land, then blocks and neighborhoods; i.e., the total regional pattern is a summation of individual actions taken by property owners in response to their own development objectives within the bounds imposed by the society.

Without assuming for a moment that regional water quality control efforts would necessarily have to satisfy all the individual requirements of each component municipality, in actual practice at the present time most of the concrete pollution control work, such as the construction of physical facilities and enforcement of regulations, is still a local responsibility, particularly in the absence of adequate watershed organizations in most locations. A look, therefore, at the local planning practices, their implications, and any modifications needed is very much warranted.

The overriding consideration in this area is a simple one: sanitary improvements (sewers) provide a service to various activities, as such they are dependent upon land uses, but often they must be constructed in advance of the full aboveground development.[1] Consequently, efficiency in the design of the service systems can only be achieved if there are reliable guidelines supplied by the entire comprehensive planning effort for the community.

THE EFFECT OF WATER QUALITY CONTROL ON COMMUNITY DEVELOPMENT

The fundamental question that arises at the very beginning of a discussion regarding the planning implications in the waste control area is whether in fact sewerage and sanitation work has any significant or even noticeable impact on regional and community structure.

Starting with the broadest considerations, we can observe that today or in the recent past no settlement of any size has been limited in its expansion by waste disposal considerations, nor has any municipality regarded this as a restraint. Yet, the above is not a very convincing argument. It can be suggested that a number of places currently suffering extreme pollution *should* have thought about these consequences, and that as urbanization becomes more intensive at many other locations this criterion will become a meaningful factor. Nor is it enough to say that our technology should be able to cope with any type and amount of waste since obviously it cannot, within a realistic cost structure. Therefore, the conclusion has

[1] One of the principal advantages stressed in the presentations discussing the recently proposed "Experimental City" of 250,000 population in Minnesota is that the new city will have a finite size and, therefore, all services can be constructed below ground, initially, and with proper dimensions, because the future loads can be precisely calculated.

to be that, while waste disposal is not likely to impose restraints in the foreseeable future on city growth at most places if proper management practices are followed, it is a consideration that should be incorporated in national, regional, and local policy determinations if overall efficiency in the use of all resources is to be achieved.

A further item for investigation is the relationship between purity standards and patterns of settlement. There does not seem to be a very tangible cause and effect here in physical terms. Under any given standard of living, many other social and economic considerations exert a more powerful and overwhelming influence over the layout and structure of a community than waste disposal requirements. The latter aspects will only emerge as highly visible features if purity standards change within an otherwise largely static situation. This then requires ripping up of streets, finding locations for treatment facilities, dislocation of established activities, changes in density patterns, and other disruptive actions. Since such instances are encountered repeatedly in most cities, the point is rather clear: Flexibility in urban planning, design, and construction is highly desirable, especially when technological systems exposed to obsolescence are involved.

The next area of inquiry is related to urban structure and development patterns, i.e., the relative distribution of specific land uses and various density zones. The New York Regional Plan Association has stated that "different patterns of urban growth do not seem to change waste management costs sufficiently to justify basing a regional plan solely on the differences." [2]

This statement is most probably true if the examination is limited to treatment only: A given population and inventory of economic activities would produce largely comparable amounts of waste under any reasonably different city layout. But the assertion cannot possibly be correct if collection and transport costs are included. And they should be incorporated in the calculations since, as was shown earlier, they can involve considerable amounts of money. The same population distributed at low density will certainly require much greater expenditures than if they were concentrated. Likewise, dis-

[2] Reference 145, p. 9.

posal costs—the finding of appropriate sites for disposal and waste transport thereto—are affected by the physical configuration of the city. Unfortunately, however, not enough data is yet available to be very precise in this area and to allow accurate estimates.

The term "solely" in the above quote is not necessary since no plan can be based on just one or a few considerations. It has never been suggested that waste management aspects should be a primary determinant in plan preparation, but the time has come when they should be recognized as *one* of the input elements. A comprehensive plan must thus be drawn and formulated with a clear understanding of the waste generation factors, of collection and treatment needs and possibilities, and of the impact that unremoved wastes may have on residents, economic activity, and the natural environment.

Another item of planning concern is found at a more local scale: the situation of activities in relation to each other in order to avoid mutual interference through the generation of pollution. This subject is discussed further in the following chapters, as are the deterministic results of specific improvements on urban development.

Finally, in summarizing the effects of waste management on planning activity, it must be stated again that environmental quality control is a much broader responsibility than can be encompassed even under the most generous definition of urban planning, and it is a task which demands the participation of many disciplines. The waste management approach as a distinct concept appears to be the proper form of attack; urban planning, however, can help in this effort, be an integral part of it, and be influenced by it to a considerable degree.

PROFESSIONAL RESPONSIBILITIES

The most important elements in the waste control field today are the overwhelming magnitude of the problem, and the need for intensive work. Who is going to do this work? Sanitary engineers, public health administrators, physicians, politicians? All of them, certainly, but also the planners. That is, the professionals who can take a comprehensive view of geographic and functional systems in an objective and rational manner weigh the various possible alternatives within the available resource limits and give reliable advice to decision makers.

It is also, however, a woeful fact that few planners have the technical competence to make meaningful evaluations beyond the intelligent layman's level. Thus, not infrequently proposals toward pollution control advanced in planning reports have been met with scorn by sanitation experts who, while not necessarily taking a broad view, can point to embarrassing gaps in specialized knowledge. Or, conversely, general waste disposal studies have been made without the participation of local planning agencies.

The first problem that planners face in asking for a closer participation in the waste control work is the question of overlapping and entrenched, if not conflicting, professional responsibilities, primarily as exercised by the engineering and, to a certain extent, the medical or public health specialists. The currently emerging concern of engineers as to their role in the community and regional planning effort has resulted in a number of statements from them which demand an almost exclusive leadership position for engineers in general planning and certainly in such areas as sanitary control. The necessity for the participation of such and similar specialized professions in planning cannot be denied, but it can also be suggested that sanitary engineering is too important to be left to the engineers alone. If nothing else, the community-building impact of sewer improvements is far-reaching and quite permanent, transcending immediate public health objectives.

It is not, certainly, implied that planners should become engineers too on top of all their other required proficiencies. Yet it must be recognized that planners in exercising their coordinating and advisory functions at several levels of government must have a grasp of the problems in waste disposal, of the available control methods and systems, and of their impact and cost factors. The increasing public concern with this crucial aspect of urban livability supports such attitude.

Briefly, planners are already specifically involved in a number of activities where they exert direct or indirect influence in environmental quality determinations; such participation may be more extensive in the future. First, they simply should have enough technical knowledge to be able to talk intelligently to, and evaluate broadly the detailed findings and proposals of, such specialists as sanitary engineers and public health experts performing their traditional duties. Interdisciplinary communications would be more than a minor benefit in many instances.

Second, by virtue of their position near the elected executive, planners are called upon to make decisions or give advice in the waste control area through proposed master plans, redevelopment schemes, regional policy formulations, and urban service extensions. A part of this general task is the very common need for an inventory report, i.e., a listing and review of facilities currently in operation in the municipality. Needless to say, this simple recording job, not to speak of evaluation of system adequacy, demands a minimum level of competence and familiarity with sewage collection and disposal methods. Expertise in administrative and financial aspects as related to waste control is perhaps even more important.

Third, planners are often required to make specific decisions with respect to waste disposal and may even be involved in certain types of simple, but detailed, design. The most common example of this is subdivision plats which are reviewed and revised in accordance with, among other things, environmental health considerations, construction of septic tanks, and provision of communal services. A somewhat related task is the drafting of ordinances, such as subdivision regulations, which include clauses concerning waste disposal, and whose preparation requires not only a general understanding of the theoretical possibilities in sewage disposal but also an ability to relate such knowledge to local conditions.

Last, but not least, there is the wide field of public education and persuasion and the guidance of sanitation projects from their inception through the administrative and legal labyrinths to final effectuation. Quite often, this too becomes the planners' responsibility.

All this can be summarized in a few statements. The team approach to urban problems and planning activity as a direct consequence of the increasing complexity of urban life, and the emergence of various specialists and experts with more intensive but also more focused knowledge, demands that there be a few professionals who can integrate the expertise of others in a balanced approach toward the development of a community or a region. In addition, environmental quality is becoming one of the most direct concerns of planners and public administrators as demanded by the public at large.

STUDY-DESIGN-CONSTRUCTION SEQUENCE

Planning for watershed or community pollution control systems in its organization does not differ at all from the basic sequence of any other planning or decision-making project:

1. Identification of objectives—determination of goals,
2. Translation of objectives into specific criteria or standards,
3. Preparation of plans, proposals, and action programs,
4. Evaluation and testing of the anticipated consequences of the plan, and
5. Organization of the means of effectuation.

The necessary modifications to this very general format are ones of emphasis and technical detail only.

For any given locality, the investigation and planning work for liquid waste control facilities may be accomplished basically through three avenues: (1) a general master plan study which includes among other considerations utility services, (2) a special study conducted to analyze sanitary needs and conditions, (3) an engineering design study for the purpose of building a system. In the first case, the study, at least theoretically, starts with no preconceived notions toward the needs and may recommend sewer improvements in balance with other community requirements. In the second case, the simple fact that a special study is initiated usually indicates that a problem exists, and therefore, the investigation has a point of view built into it. In the third case, a decision to build has been made and the work is focused toward actual design.

It would be convenient and satisfying if one could state that a general planning study usually establishes the need for a water quality control system, defines objectives, and sets the dimensions of the work; that this is followed by a focused investigation of the problem which refines and specifies all policy aspects and objectives;

and that all is brought to effectuation via an engineering project which supplies the acutal working drawings.

Needless to say, this idealized progression toward a goal does not occur often in real life. There have been occasions where the residents themselves have taken the initiative to campaign for a better environment, thereby indicating clearly that the responsible officials have neglected their duties or have chosen not to exert positive leadership. More often, however, studies by professionals pointing out the need for improvements have been shelved for political or financial reasons by the public authorities, or the proposals have been defeated by the electorate, usually on a cost basis. In many cases, the successful construction of a new sewer system is the culmination of numerous studies and reports going back many years. The theoretical study sequence has also been altered in recent years by the direct or indirect participation of state and Federal governments. This introduces a few new complications in the administrative phases of the work, but assures greater possibility of effectuation.[3] Similarly, regional and watershed agencies have begun to assume an active role and can be expected in the future to establish quality standards and a framework within which each local effort will have to fit.

The remainder of this section will be devoted to an attempt to outline a desirable work sequence including the required efforts by various professions and agencies.[4] The following description will be kept within the bounds of currently established practices; further improvements in procedures and approaches which would require considerable modifications will be suggested in another section.

Assuming that legal authority (enabling legislation) exists for the agency under consideration to work in the sanitary field, the first task can be defined as the establishment of the need for water quality and liquid waste disposal systems. However, since this is a foregone conclusion in most actual instances, the work can be directed immediately toward policy determinations with respect to environmental standards, extent and scope of control systems, and financial feasi-

[3] See page 111.
[4] The actual details, scope, and problems of each step will not be discussed here, but can be found in the appropriate sections throughout this monograph.

bility. The primary responsibility here rests with the elected officials; yet they need support and advice from various professionals: sanitary engineers, public health specialists, administrators, financial experts, and planners. During this phase, which is geared toward the definition of objectives, the public education and information work of local residents may also start. Contacts have to be established with various local and higher level agencies which have an interest or responsibility in public sanitation to obtain information, to establish good workable relations, and to take into account, or at least be aware of, their requirements.

The background information to justify the preliminary but fundamental decisions may come from special purpose analyses, from regionwide investigations, or from local master plan studies. Comparing the many actual examples of this type of survey that have been done for communities in the United States, different emphases can be noted in each report depending on whether the health, public works, planning, or some other department prepared the study. However, authorship and even orientation is not too important provided that the report can supply useful and well-reasoned information. Items included here will be the conventional aspects of population projections in aggregate and for detailed drainage subareas, anticipated or planned location of residential, industrial, and commercial districts with their intensity and sewage flow rate estimates on a per capita or acreage basis, and other social and economic investigations. Planners can usually make their greatest contribution during this phase since the decisions reached here must rest on community-wide, coordinated and forward-looking aspects, not just technical knowledge.

Following this, or in parallel, an inventory study is required which records precisely the environmental and physical conditions (geology, topography, drainage patterns) in the area and gives also a detailed description and evaluation of any existing utility systems that will have an effect on the contemplated improvements. Specific data on present deficiencies and localized excess capacities of available sewerage systems will be particularly important. If this information is included in a general planning report, it should be prepared in collaboration with a qualified engineer. If the data is compiled by engineers in a special report, the planners should participate to include considerations which overlap several areas of concern. An engineering consultant, particularly for smaller municipalities, will most likely enter during this stage.

Specific policy determinations can be made at this point as guidance for further work, i.e., a program for design can be prepared outlining precisely the dimensions, level of service, cost factors, coverage, and components of the proposed system. The work done locally may be heavily influenced by regulations and policies established at higher levels of government, such as state and Federal water quality standards and requirements for financial aid. A regional watershed agency may also exist and be empowered to exert any level of control over local operations.

It is rather clear that at each succeeding step in the study sequence technical specialists assume an increasingly dominant role until studies are reached which are purely and exclusively within the engineers' province.

The next phase would be devoted to the preparation of alternative schematic plans whose primary purpose is to test the feasibility of various approaches and their ability to satisfy objectives and standards. Again, this is a collaborative task between planners, engineers, and other experts so that it becomes impossible to state who has the main responsibility. It is not a purely engineering job. From the several alternatives, a "most likely" solution will begin to emerge. The extent of the system, its major elements, basic structure, and character, as well as cost and staging will be defined and estimated during this phase. The available methods of financing will also be evaluated. The decisions again, of course, will be made by the public officials.

The plan should be ready now to go formally before the public. In most instances the size of the project and the need to borrow construction funds, not only the advisability of informing the electorate, demands such action. As in all other similar instances, a thorough public education and information campaign is indicated. Here too the planner should assume a leading role in explaining and justifying the overall concept, the significance of the solution, and its beneficial impact.

If the public reaction, including a possible referendum, is favorable, detailed construction plans can be prepared. If these are already available, designs can be refined and final construction specifications written. The planner will have little to do during this phase, except perhaps to consult with the designers when departures from previous determinations appear warranted. With accurate cost estimates available, methods of financing can be selected, funds obtained, construction bids received, contractors selected and hired, and construction can start.

As was stated before, this is a somewhat simplified and idealized sequence. Under actual conditions any number of modifications may have to be made or may appear justified. For example, quite often detailed engineering drawings are prepared before the public is informed and consulted, or such designs are on file from previous studies. But, all in all, the above steps appear to be a logical progression with the least amount of potentially wasted effort and risk, and they fit easily not only within the current administrative procedures but also within the accepted attitudes toward sanitary control work.

THE CHOICE OF SYSTEMS IN SUBURBIA

At the present time, working within the technological and economic restraints with respect to liquid waste disposal, the core problem facing local planners and public decision makers regarding any given town without liquid waste control improvements or the newer sections of an existing community, particularly the developing suburban areas, is the selection of a suitable sewerage system—broadly speaking: municipal network or individual septic tanks? More precisely, at what density does it become feasible or necessary to require a communal system instead of allowing property owners to rely on septic tanks? [5] There is widespread uncertainty, and it is reflected as such in planning reports, as to the appropriate system for zones of specific density to achieve any desired environmental quality.

Since a great portion of the city building activity in the United

[5] J. A. Salvato reports in "Problems of Wastewater Disposal in Suburbia," *Public Works,* March 1964, pp. 120–21, 172–78 (reference 100) that, in 1960, 23 million out of the total metropolitan population of 113 million and nationwide 4 out of 10 Americans were served by septic tanks.

States in the recent past has been (and will be in the foreseeable future) in the form of fringe area development, i.e., subdivisions built on formerly rural land, the provision of utility service in such areas has assumed critical importance. It is certainly not the only problem, but it is a most dramatic one having a long-range impact. This is particularly so because the suburban areas are characterized by the dominance of small political units which are inherently ill-adapted for the provision of efficient engineering services,[6] have not been equipped to offer even minimal public works improvements, and are settled by families that expect and demand high-level services.

It is not always reasonable to say that only municipal systems can be permitted since anything else is bound to pollute water or soil. Costs and habits are involved and, as has been discussed, certain individual systems are acceptable under strict control in areas with suitable characteristics.

The search of available literature will not give any answers to this question. The hints and assumptions which are found scattered here and there are not reliable since they are not backed up with adequate justification and technical proof. For example, suggestions that 1-family or 2-family per acre density is the threshold below which septic tanks are permissible, or that public sewers are rarely justified in areas with densities below 2,500 to 5,000 persons per square mile can be highly misleading in any particular case, although they may have some use as preliminary indicators.

It all depends on the substrata conditions on the spot and locally defined levels of desired sanitation. There is no universally applicable answer, except to say that communal systems are always to be preferred. If individual disposal appears to be justified, however, a detailed examination is required. In any case, here is an area where careful research could fill a gap in knowledge confronting the planner.

The unwise practices of the twenties and thirties when municipalities constructed streets and utilities as demanded by private developers have, of course, ceased. The results were premature subdivisions characterized by the presence of expensive public improvements and scattered houses. The strain on the municipal budget, as well as ad-

---

[6] The administrative, control, and operative features related to this item are discussed in Chapter 6, Financial Aspects.

verse public reaction—old residents had to finance the improvements for new residents—gave rise to the current general requirements that each subdivider be responsible for the construction of streets and utilities in his development. Furthermore, the ring of development around most cities has moved in the meantime beyond the central city boundaries to formerly rural areas which would not have the financial base anyway for the construction of extensive utility systems.

Under such conditions, the initiative rests with the developer. Naturally, he would select those types of improvements which suit best his purposes, represented by maximum profit and flexibility of capital investment. This is not to say that all subdividers are only interested in a quick profit, it is simply a statement of the rules of the game for financial survival. Consequently, from this point of view, the individual sewage disposal systems offer the greatest advantages: they do not tie up huge sums of money, they do not have to be built prior to house construction, their costs can be passed on to the home buyer directly and without much argument, they can be built gradually and, as has been demonstrated by some unscrupulous developers, they operate quite satisfactorily during the first year or so under any circumstances. If they fail later, the original builder may have moved on.[7]

Septic tanks and leaching fields are not easy to inspect during construction to assure proper standards unless the public agencies keep the development under continuous surveillance. The experiences of the recent past in this area prove that caution on the part of the municipal authorities is eminently justifiable.

Another crucial point to consider before allowing the construction of septic tanks in any given area is the stability of the section in terms of development. There have been numerous instances in the recent past where densities have intensified soon after the original settlement, and this has either resulted in unacceptable sanitary conditions or has necessitated the belated construction of municipal sewers. In the latter case, the septic tank systems have been a complete economic loss since they have no salvage value, and the building of a collection

---

[7] A remedy of this may be the requirement of a performance bond by the builder to guarantee the septic tank systems for a number of years against failure. Such 5-year bond is now required by New York City (Staten Island) and has been met, predictably, by builders' protests.

network under paved streets, in the presence of traffic, has been much more expensive and inconvenient than it would have been if the system had been constructed at the beginning. This expense can easily be three times the original cost.

Parenthetically, it can also be mentioned that there is a danger that the house owner may have to pay a third time if the municipal system is later upgraded into a comprehensive but substantially different regionwide pollution control network. To avoid such repetitive waste of investment, flexibility in construction within a realistic long-range plan is clearly indicated.

On the other hand, if the density remains the same—large lots as required for seepage fields—but the community recognizes later the need for a higher level of sanitary services, provision of a collection network may be quite uneconomical because of the need for long lines accommodating only scattered inlet points.

There have been numerous instances during the great housing shortage after World War II where developers were content to provide only primitive cesspools which are now outlawed in practically all communities having any kind of health or subdivision regulations. This also illustrates further the uninspiring history in the development of public controls, especially in the environmental area, in this country which has been geared toward stopping crisis situations and abuses after they have appeared. Technology and building practices have always been a few steps ahead of the regulations available to the public to preserve its environment at a level found desirable during any time period.

Since in recent decades most of the urban development has taken place in suburban areas characterized by small political units, these shortcomings have been particularly visible. Under such circumstances, short-range solutions have been traditionally favored; to a large extent, this has been the consequence of a shortage of funds and competent personnel.

Be that as it may, generally speaking, there are today adequate controls in most urbanized or urbanizing areas of the country. Theoretically, these provide ample protection to the community and users of septic tank systems. The Federal government (particularly the U.S. Public Health Service) and various state and county health departments have developed and adopted standards and regulations which can do the job. Local enforcement, however, is another matter.

A developer may be forced into the provision of a communal system by any of several factors:

1. The local ordinances may simply demand such action and this may, in turn, be the result of two conditions: (a) a municipal system is in existence reasonably near so that the subdivision can be connected without undue expense, and/or (b) the community has decided to enforce superior environmental standards which can be achieved with a regular collection network and treatment plant.

2. The subsoil conditions are not suitable for septic tank disposal (high ground water level or impermeable soil) and therefore only overall systems can cope with the sanitation problems. (Incidentally, this would be the strongest, although not necessarily the only, justification for point 1(b) above.)

3. The home buyers, who have become recently more selective and knowledgeable, may recognize the long-range advantages of a public system. Or, to put it another way, the developer may find it a marketing asset to provide sewerage networks which can support his claim of having created a "planned community" —a label which is currently a strong selling feature.

If the builder decides, or is required, to construct a sewer system, a number of new problems surface creating difficulties in the achievement of this the preferred solution.[8] The primary one is financing, which demands a large investment in site improvement cost before any return can be obtained. Borrowing specifically for sewer improvements is not feasible since the developer does not want or is not allowed by law to operate the system as a self-supporting enterprise after construction. Thus he can offer no security to lending institutions on this improvement alone. The expenses must be absorbed by the entire development, as has been done in some large projects[9] making the financial burden that much heavier for the investor.

---

[8] These problems have been discussed by D. Bogdanoff, an active builder in Westchester County, N.Y., and recognized as one of the more community minded developers, on several occasions, including an article in *The New York Times,* May 24, 1959, "Sewer Problems Vexing in Suburbs."

[9] Reston, Va., and Columbia, Md., for example.

The partial use of public funds would be a solution, but this participation cannot usually be expected from the local government. Federal or state aids again emerge as the potential means having the ability to consolidate greater funds, and to distribute them according to needs of the larger society or at least the region.

It is to be noted that the above considerations apply primarily when the developer has to construct both a collection system and a treatment plant or a very long outfall sewer to the nearest public system. In cases where only laterals are needed, which can be tied directly into an existing system, the costs are directly comparable to septic tank construction expenses, and no public financial aids need to be considered.

SITE AND SIZE OF TREATMENT PLANTS

If a comprehensive municipal system is proposed for a community, two factors will be of direct interest to the planner: the location and acreage required for treatment plants to allow proper siting and sizing of this facility in the community plan.

Obviously, the site should be located at the lowest point within the service district to minimize the need for pumping stations from the gravity flow network. It should also be directly adjacent to the last downstream sewage generator to avoid the necessity for long trunk sewers. The location most often will have to be within the political boundaries of the community served to avoid administrative problems. Thus the plant is among the few urban activities whose location is strictly dictated by economic and engineering considerations.

Since there is practically no flexibility in this respect, the planning problem becomes one of the determination of compatible neighboring uses. It has to be stated that theoretically a well-run treatment plant need not generate any smells. But, because no plant can be expected to be kept continuously in completely immaculate condition, localized and diffuse gaseous emissions will be given off occasionally from the open tanks. Consequently, the location of activities which house, employ, or attract people is precluded within certainly several hundred feet of a large municipal treatment plant. This distance is about the best that can be expected in an urban situation and should provide adequate protection practically all the time. Many existing plants in large cities do not offer even this much of a buffer. There is, however, a considerable element of risk involved, because some unforeseeable breakdowns in the operations may result in an overpowering stench which, even if it is of a short duration, will cause a violent public reaction. Under such a crisis situation, with the wind in the right direction, even a thousand feet of separation will not be enough. But the crisis itself is avoidable.

An expensive but often justifiable alternative in cases where no choice of location exists may be complete enclosure, containing any olfactory and esthetic nuisances. The open plant can be screened visually, in recognition of the psychological aspects of the improvement, but the unfortunate experiences in the recent past with billowing mounds of detergent foam, which could surmount most obstacles, show that sometimes even these safeguards are not adequate.

Transportation access is not a major problem since the plant attracts a negligible flow of workers or material on surface streets. The only exception may be the disposal of the sludge which, depending upon the process used, can result in a light but potentially messy truck movement. A number of small plants sell or give away dried sludge as fertilizer; this has to be carted away. In New York City all plants are on navigable waterways because the digested sludge is taken by barge for dumping into the ocean.

As a result of these considerations, two types of surrounding land uses appear proper. Heavy industrial districts may be one, where any possible nuisance generated by the treatment plant will not interfere with other operations which may produce even greater nuisances. However, while this has been the traditional approach in the past, the changing character of industrial districts themselves through the incorporation of environmental controls, or even the removal of the heaviest activities from the built-up areas proper, suggest that treatment plants located in industrial areas be also carefully designed.

The other suitable neighbors, paradoxical as it may sound, are recreational areas and parks. They and sewage plants seek waterfront locations, and there is little impact on the park by a treatment plant since a built-in buffer strip, adequate distances, and visual screens between the plant and well-used recreational locations can be provided easily.

The question of acreage requirements is much more difficult to resolve. Most of the space allocated for a treatment plant need not be taken up by tanks and equipment, but can often be devoted to landscaped areas and buffer strips. The size, therefore, has to be determined from inside out: first the functional components of the plant should be designed and laid out, then surrounded with protective areas; finally adjustments should be made according to available space.

The best that can be done here is to give a few examples of the amounts of space actually used; these vary quite widely:

Plant name and location	Type of treatment	Capacity	Acreage
New Paltz, N.Y.	Modified Imhoff tanks	0.4 mgd	1 acre
Woodridge, N.Y.	Trickling filters	0.9 mgd	4 acres
Los Gallinos, Marin Co.	2-stage trickling filter	3.7 mgd	5 acres
Plattsburgh, N.Y.	Primary with sludge digest.	4 mgd	6 acres
San Rafael, Marin Co.	Activated sludge	8 mgd	2 acres
Irvington, Alameda Co.	Trickling filter	10.5 mgd	12.5 acres
North Point, San Francisco	Primary	40 mgd	10 acres
Virginia Key, Miami, Fla.	High-rate activ. sludge	47 mgd plus provis. for 50% exp.	68 acres
Brooklyn Navy Yard, New York City (Proposed)	Activ. sludge and refuse incinerator	50 mgd + 5000 tons of refuse	24 acres
Puetz Road, Milwaukee	Activ. sludge (to be constr.) incl. sludge lagoons	120 mgd	108 acres

Plant name and location	Type of treatment	Capacity	Acreage
Bowery Bay, New York City	Activ. sludge	120 mgd	20 acres
Mill Creek, Cincinnati	Activ. sludge (to be constr.)	120 mgd (avg) 360 mgd (max)	60 acres
Hudson River, New York City (Proposed)	Activ. sludge	150 to 220 mgd	20 to 40 acres
East Bay Munic. Utility Distr., Oakland	Primary	290 mgd	28 acres

As a general rule of thumb, it can be suggested that for any municipal plant a minimum plot of 5 acres has to be reserved in all cases, even for population sizes around 10,000, to provide a satisfactory buffer zone. For the population range around 25,000, 10 acres appear to be an adequate land allocation; 50–60,000 people can be served by a plant taking up 15 acres; beyond that size, any general figures become meaningless because of the great number of variations possible in plant design and layout.

COMMUNITY-BUILDING SIGNIFICANCE

GENERAL CONSIDERATIONS. While it is a universally held belief that modern sewer systems improve materially the health, sanitary, and livability aspects of any community, for the public in most localities there are two major obstacles that must be overcome before such improvements can be effectuated.

The first is purely financial. Any collection and treatment system is an expensive undertaking which requires the expenditure of large sums for the laying of an extensive underground pipe network, and the construction of a complex purification plant. And this money has to be spent within a relatively short period that can be spread only to a certain extent by borrowing and the issuance of bonds.

It is rarely easy to convince the taxpayers of an old, low-density community, traditionally dependent on individual disposal systems, that they should strain their municipal budget to build improvements which seemingly help only the newcomers. To construct new sewers in an already built-up area is an even more difficult and costly endeavor.

In either case, the treatment of sewage by any one municipality will primarily benefit the downstream neighbors, not so much the community itself. Historical evidence has shown that voluntary pollution control efforts based on civic conscience are thus highly rare and unreliable. Since the costs cannot at present be traded off between any two communities, enforcement of standards by higher agencies achieves almost the same effect, because expenditures are required from everybody—thus a form of equalization is in effect. This, coupled with financial aid from the state and Federal governments, represents the main leverage for achieving a better environment. There may also be a gradually emerging recognition of areawide responsibilities, although examples are still rather scarce, an awareness of economies possible through metropolitan cooperation, and a concern with regional recreation facilities, all of which should foster and accelerate pollution control work.

Secondly, there is the whole question of change in community character which has a reciprocal cause and effect relationship: a sewer system is not only required because of dense development, its presence encourages dense development. In fact, considerations of operational efficiency require a maximum utilization of the system. Similarly, commercial activities and industrial establishments seek locations which are served by utilities, thereby changing the milieu and appearance of a community further. On the other hand, such taxpayers can help to carry the costs of sewer improvements.

Thus, from the point of view of any small community, particularly if it is peripheral to a large center, a decision to build or not to build a sewer system is not only a question of environmental standards. It is also an irrevocable commitment to a certain way of life in all respects. As such it becomes a part of the basic planning and community-building policy which cannot stand alone but must be coordinated with all other decisions with respect to such things as housing, transportation, economic base, and service facilities.

If we look at the same aspect in another way, the available level of service reflects the local attitude toward sanitation standards as modified by the community's ability to pay; it classifies the area as to its desirability for new residences, factories, and other improvements. The existing system is a direct consequence of past policies and attitudes; present policies and attitudes will result in a future system with commensurate service quality. Yet, the traditional approach toward the building of sewer improvements has been, and still is, to provide them where they are most obviously needed or where a crisis situation may unmistakably arise in their absence.

The most expedient approach in many instances has been to allow individual sewage disposal systems, thus seemingly reaching a solution which does not require any direct municipal expenditures. Such a decision not only can cause unfortunate sanitary and functional consequences, as was discussed previously, but it may also have a detrimental and permanent effect on future municipal expenditures. For example, it may encourage the influx of unscrupulous builders who will leave developments with built-in liabilities, and it will foster leapfrog settlements, with vacant space in-between, which are bound to result in higher costs for all public services.

Sewerage has been regarded as a service which follows the fact of development. Yet, it can be suggested that the provision of any utility and public improvement can have a positive causative effect and can serve as one of the guiding elements in the organization of a community and the deliberate channelization of its development. This last aspect, if adopted as a conscious policy, can add a new dimension in the entire planning effort for a municipality.

The above statements have to be presented as a hypothesis, since carefully documented proofs of such actual occurrences in a sequential manner are not available in a clear enough form, and extensive field research and analysis of the growth of specific cities as related to their sanitary systems' development would be required to supply an unimpeachable answer.

Even more important, under a largely permissive attitude on the part of the government in allowing subdivisions and developments to locate quite freely with only a few restrictions in the public health and waste control field, the cause and effect relationships in the sanitary field are submerged by other locational considerations and may be impossible to isolate. In areas where inadequate septic tank systems are tolerated, little correlation, most likely, will be found.

Nevertheless, the fact that past practices have been deficient and that, consequently, available evidence may be inconclusive does not defeat the proposal. It can be postulated that the constructive use of sanitary regulations and provision of facilities can and must receive very serious attention within the context of local planning as another, hitherto not fully explored, means of settlement organization. It involves two push-pull aspects: (1) major improvements (interceptor lines, treatment plants) at proper locations must be provided by the community, and (2) development at unsuitable sites, either because of sanitary considerations or general policy, must be prohibited. Evidence shows that if only one of these two features are present the results are minimal.

If these, as well as the other elements mentioned above, are true for a local jurisdiction, they are equally valid for a region. The impact of a total watershed plan, if effectuated, can range from the change in the market value of any single parcel to the modification of areawide quality of life.

The physical planning process under the above approach can be envisioned as first the positioning of major collector lines as determinants of growth—their location can be regarded as a policy decision with respect to the desired future structure of the community within a comprehensive and rational plan. It can be assumed that the presence of such utilities will encourage the development of the areas served, particularly if other sections are under restraints. Consequently, future land uses can be distributed, taking into account all the factors which "open up an area" or channelize development. Once the total amount of development and its density is determined, the layout and capacity of laterals and smaller service lines can be designed.

In other words, general policy has to be established as to which areas can and should be built up; the major services are then made available to these areas to assure such development; finally, the anticipated land uses are serviced by local connections. Thus, the presence and availability of utilities can be regarded as an inducement and attraction to development, while their detailed design at the zone or block level is a purely secondary service task.

The actual construction of sewers can follow the same sequence as outlined above for planning: major trunk lines constructed first by the public, and laterals in most suburban areas built in parallel with other development by private entrepreneurs within overall specifications.

The final aspect of the problem in planning for waste control improvements is the sequencing of construction in case of growth as illustrated in Fig. 9. Assuming that a situation where actual population exceeds facility capacity should not be allowed, the timing of construction is dependent on both the expected population size and a meaningful plant size to be built and operated as a unit. If this module is a large one, there will be long periods with idle and wasteful capacity; if the modules can be made smaller (perhaps unitized extensions to an existing plant), the available capacity can approximate much closer the service demand curve with reduced slack. A crucial feature of all the above is, of course, the lead time which is taken up by design and construction before a plant can be placed in operation at the proper instant. Careful planning and scheduling, as well as reliable population estimates, are again required.

PERMANENCY OF IMPROVEMENTS. As was noted previously, there are two factors which are of great importance in the discussion of the community-building significance of sewerage systems: the improvements are expensive, and they last a long time.

The permanency of the improvements is the subject for further examination on the following pages. One of the strongest reasons, among several others, why most of the cities in Germany were rebuilt after World War II on the same inefficient and ancient street layouts was the survival of the underground utility lines. This preserved investment could not be ignored. Because of the considerable expense involved in the changing and moving of buried service pipes, even under normal circumstances, sewers have to be regarded as fixed for most reconstruction projects. Furthermore, any restructuring of an existing system can usually involve only a limited segment, and the

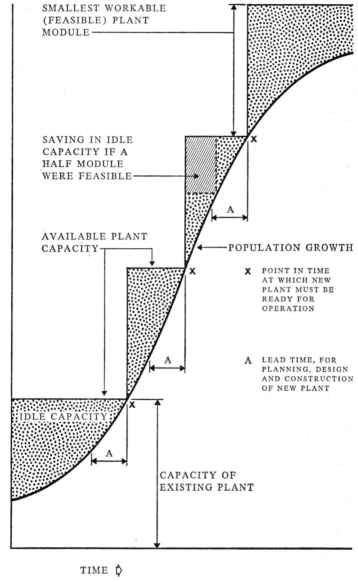

SMALLEST WORKABLE
(FEASIBLE) PLANT
MODULE

SAVING IN IDLE
CAPACITY IF A
HALF MODULE
WERE FEASIBLE

AVAILABLE PLANT
CAPACITY

POPULATION GROWTH

X POINT IN TIME
   AT WHICH NEW
   PLANT MUST BE
   READY FOR
   OPERATION

A LEAD TIME, FOR
   PLANNING, DESIGN
   AND CONSTRUCTION
   OF NEW PLANT

IDLE CAPACITY

CAPACITY OF
EXISTING PLANT

POPULATION OF COMMUNITY
AND
CAPACITY OF SEWAGE PLANT

TIME

FIGURE 9

new section has to fit within the old framework. Thus a self-perpetuating layout is almost assured. It follows, therefore, that street changes, which should be easier tasks because surface improvements are less costly to remove or replace, become quite difficult since street alignments are ordinarily associated with colinear utility lines. The usual solution under such circumstances is to leave the utilities where they are, retaining an easement along the surface for maintenance purposes, and relocating the vehicular roadway only.

Such rigidity imposed by physical service facilities appears to be at odds with the currently emerging approach toward urban planning, which is beginning to stress flexibility of execution within the scope of reasonable, long-range policy guidelines. The basis for this new attitude generally, and particularly with respect to utilities and other urban mechanical services, is the simple fact that it is difficult to foresee what the specific future requirements will be; it is also impossible to predict what form and shape the actual future improvements will take or what the actual demands will be. Translating this into sewerage terms, we can advance two thoughts.

First, systems which could be split into semi-independent components, and thus function together or separately depending on cirsumstances, would provide a great amount of freedom in the expansion or replacement of parts of the overall network. For example, each city zone and neighborhood, if not each building, could be serviced by a complete and separate waste disposal system. The great obstacle here is economic feasibility, but the recent emergence of package plants points toward a possible modification of the present situation.

Second, the archaic, if not ridiculous, practice of burying a pipe which, as everybody knows, will at some time need exhumation for repairs, could also benefit from some new thinking. Time and again suggestions have been made to construct utility tunnels on whose walls any utility lines could be hung, thus being always accessible for inspection and repair. It has never, however, been tried in a large scale for public utilities, and several reasons can be listed for the inability of this idea to attract support. The tunnel itself, of course, would represent a heavy investment; the initial cost is bound to be much greater than all the original trench digging for the separate utility lines. There are technical problems: a bursting water pipe can short-circuit power lines, and leaking sewage might possibly pollute drinking water. Some utilities flow under pressure; others must respect gravity. However, the greatest obstacle appears to be the splintered responsibilities of various utility companies and agencies. Very often each service or groups of services in the United States are provided by completely autonomous organizations, and there is little exchange of information, not to speak of active cooperation.

Yet, regardless of the above difficulties, which are real but not unsurmountable, it is interesting to consider what effect such a system could have on the physical layout, organization, and operation of city districts.

The utility tunnels could act as the fundamental service, circulation, and distribution system of the city. They would remain fixed but their contents could be changed in size and type and could incorporate certain mechanical movement systems, such as goods distribution. Because the useful life of the tunnel itself would have to be measured in centuries, the configuration of this network would have to be simple and basic, perhaps a grid-iron. Spacing between tunnels would depend on development density; their size would have to be large enough to carry any future loads. There would be almost complete freedom of activity distribution on the surface with the "plug-in" city concept[10] within reach. This would allow planners and designers to regard most of the surface improvements as temporary, which they actually are as proven by the replacement frequency of buildings within old city core areas. The utility network would act as the permanent "guts" of the city for which considerable investment could be justified. This seemingly revolutionary idea is nothing more than the extension of current practices in the provision of mechanical equipment in buildings (utility chases and tunnels within single structures) to a larger scale and the full exploitation of our technological capabilities in city building.

Concluding this section, one more speculative note is in order: all of the above may not be necessary if an operable and cheap water purification and recirculation apparatus can be developed that would

---

[10] See the recent proposal by the Archigram group; also *Architecture: Action and Plan* by Peter Cook (New York: Reinhold Publishing Corp., 1967). The Minnesota "Experimental City" proposals are very similar.

be economical for a single building or even apartment. The inherent inefficiency of a small unit would have to be balanced against its ability to eliminate extensive water distribution and sewage collection pipelines. But here too, the answer suggests itself: separate units in areas of low density; community systems in dense urban concentrations, provided, of course, that density levels can be fixed for a reasonable amount of time so that conversions from one system to another are not called for.

SUGGESTED RESEARCH

Historical study of the effects of utilities on urban development.

Development of a defined planning approach utilizing service improvements as one of the determinants and organizing factors of settlement patterns.

Establishment of standard guidelines and procedures to be followed in community sewerage and sanitation studies (inventory, needs, effects).

Examination of the planning-design-construction sequence of utility improvements as to its optimum organization, place in the public decision making process, and overall methodology.

Definition of the professional responsibilities of various experts and specialists in the sanitation as well as other areas of public concern.

Study of utility planning possibilities for district redevelopment projects.

Examination of the suitability of different disposal systems under various densities and physical conditions.

Investigation of the "utility grid" as potentially the basic and permanent service system of a city.

Investigation of the effects that different urban development and settlement patterns have on waste management—generation, collection, treatment, and disposal.

8

PROBLEMS IN
DEVELOPING COUNTRIES

The discussion so far has been related to the conditions and needs of the old industrialized countries with a particular emphasis on the practice in the United States. Similar problems exist also in the newer, recently organized, and rapidly expanding societies and nations, usually referred to as the developing countries. The sanitary situation in the urbanized areas of these regions is even more serious; the solutions are more difficult to find; the conditions in most instances are getting worse. Not enough sanitation work is being done to keep pace with urban population increases, not to speak of catching up with past neglect. The World Health Organization[1] has concluded that one of the prime reasons for the critical conditions in many developing countries is that they have been in a great haste to provide potable water to residents, but have neglected or found it impossible to provide comparable facilities to handle the same water after use. Or the attraction of a new industry and the mining of materials are considered so vital that these activities are given effectively a *carte blanche* to pollute their surroundings. Irrigation works too have often been designed and built without consideration of their secondary effects: the loss of water volumes to carry off wastes or the impact of bacteria-contaminated water on fruit and vegetable crops. Water-born diseases and intestinal infections consequently are common.

[1] A committee of experts met in December 1967, to survey conditions in various countries.

The conclusion that has been reached in this study with respect to sewage disposal work is that knowledge and information is largely available on the technical and public health aspects. The problem is how to utilize it—not only to maintain sanitary conditions but also to achieve other community-building objectives—and how to apply it to areas that do not have the technical and financial capacity that is often taken for granted in countries such as the United States. Not only must the basic premises and objectives often be modified from those adopted and used in the industrialized countries, but also the technical and physical aspects of environmental planning may have a different orientation. This is a particularly significant aspect which has not always been recognized by numerous technical experts who have tried to apply standard "Western" solutions to societies with differing values, ways of life, and financial ability. It has been suggested, and rightly so in a great many cases, that the primary problem facing urban concentrations in non-industrialized countries is not housing, economic base, education, or similar concerns, but rather fundamental sanitation, i.e., the provision of an adequate supply of drinkable water and a satisfactory waste disposal system. In many instances it is a question of life or death, not to speak of human dignity and self-respect. One cannot teach a child to read if he is debilitated by diarrhea or expect a man to take great interest in improving his shelter if he has to wade through his own, his neighbors', and his animals' filth.

Sanitation needs at the survival level are about the same for any group of people, regardless of where they live and what their cultural development may be. All human beings produce the same type of bodily wastes and are affected by pollutants in the same way, biologically and medically speaking. Thus it can be said that what is good for the United States is also good for a new African or Asian republic. Yet even in the United States and Western Europe environmental quality is not always at the recognized or desired optimum but at a somewhat or considerably lower level, depending largely on the willingness of each community to pay for its waste control works. This is an even more important consideration in societies with extremely limited resources in relation to needs. In many instances developing countries have found it appropriate for the time being to attempt to achieve a degree of sanitation which only eliminates the outright threat of deaths and epidemics due to pollution, and to invest the rest of their limited funds in economic development and other similar activities.

Furthermore, the potential of public improvements (roads, water mains, and sewer lines) to structure a sprawling settlement and give it some semblance of order cannot be overemphasized, as was discussed previously. In developing countries particularly this may be the most direct, if not the only, positive means available to the local planners and officials.[2] The expenditures in community building must thus not only be gauged as to their adequacy to satisfy public health requirements, but must also be channeled and controlled as short- and long-range programs toward a permanent and viable settlement.

The planning approach has to be through a comprehensive analysis of the various considerations which have a direct or indirect bearing on the decisions with respect to community investments. The immediate need is not so much for a defined model, since adequate information is not yet available and a number of the pertinent items cannot be easily quantified, but rather for a systematic approach toward a solution, based on separate cost-benefit analyses in a sequence of steps.

It is particularly important for developing countries to have first a regional or even nationwide allocation of resources among economic development projects, which will have a largely long-range effect on the improvement of conditions, and second to have community facilities projects, which offer a tangible and immediate impact on the physical and cultural environment (see Fig. 10). Out of the second group of potential projects, sewage disposal is only one, and it has to compete for funds with such other programs as school construction, provision of medical services, and establishment of libraries.

The choices are not easy to make in attempting to achieve an equitable allocation of resources. The costs for the various projects can be estimated reasonably well, but their benefits to the community

---

[2] See, for example, the sanitary and planning studies prepared by the Hydrotechnic Corporation of New York, in association with the author, in 1965 for the cities of Tumbes, Tacna, and Trujillo in Peru, and in 1968 for Santo Domingo and Santiago in the Dominican Republic.

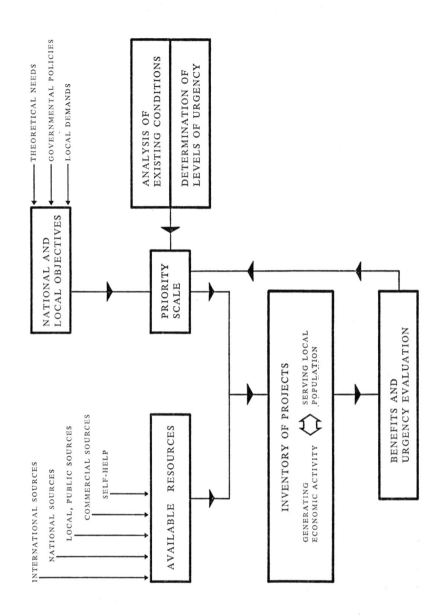

FIGURE 10

are not even comparable in a relative way, much less in strict monetary terms. If the construction expenses for a new sewer system and a new industrial district are the same, which one should be built? At the present this question can be answered only on a political basis; a more rational and scientific determination is a long way off. One cannot always build half of each because then neither may be effective; nor can it always be said that the sewer service is more important at all locations, because it answers an urgent and crucial need for each community. This improvement may have to be delayed in favor of a long-range economic benefit—provided, of course, that the survival level of sanitation has been achieved. Thus, planning has to start with a list of objectives which may ultimately be expressed at the local level as potential projects. This list has to be formulated in terms of available resources on a year-by-year basis, with a careful ranking by priorities. The funds may come from the national treasury, international loans or grants, local public sources, outside commercial investments, or local private activities. As far as sanitary improvements are concerned, they are second only to food and basic shelter, at least until a point is reached where epidemic diseases and excessive mortality rates are checked. After that, the field is open, and it can only be hoped that the decisions will be made within the framework of a regional or national resource management system.

At the local community and city level, the task is primarily to achieve a maximum return for the funds invested in specific improvements. It has to be stated again that the crucial and most difficult decision is not in the selection of the physical system, and the design of its elements within the budget limitations, but rather in the coordination of the ancillary activities and benefits. These include the satisfaction of urgent and often long-standing demands, allowing the people to recover some of the self-respect that they may have lost by moving to the city, giving a structure to neighborhoods, channelization of development into workable patterns, and similar items.

All the above can be summarized in the following chart (Fig. 11) which portrays the basic decision process, incorporating a few of the most important input requirements and output possibilities.

The features in the sanitary area that distinguish a developing country from one that is industrialized, and which have to be taken into

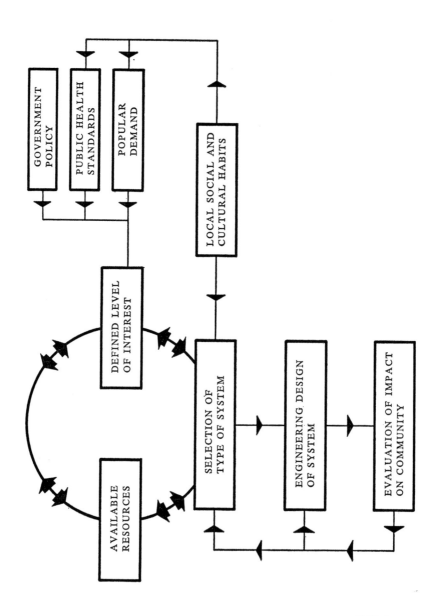

FIGURE 11

account in the structuring of an environmental control program are basically the following:

1. Limitations on resources, especially construction funds.
2. Quite often, the complete absence of any existing community system whatsoever. In the poorer sections of cities, particularly squatters' settlements, the environmental quality may be on an absolutely primitive level. This may be coupled with extremely high residential densities.
3. Lack of precise control mechanisms, including regulations, codes, administrative organizations, and even such indirect but vital elements as property definitions.
4. Incomplete data and facts of a concrete and specific nature. No one can take pride in publishing them; often there are no resources to collect them.
5. Shortage of technical skills needed for the construction, maintenance, and operation of complex systems.
6. Higher tolerance by the population of negative visual and psychological manifestations of pollution, and only limited demand for sanitary improvements by the local residents themselves since they lack a standard for comparison.

The last item, without doubt, is a temporary phenomenon which will be erased as living conditions and communications improve. Yet this feature may provide a breathing spell between the immediate construction of basic improvements and the building up of demands for refinements.

Several other characteristics can be observed in many, but not all, cities within developing countries. They result in differences in the degree of sanitary pollution but not in the kind of problems found locally. It can be observed that in most instances rural populations have evolved, over the centuries, workable communal sanitary services, habits, and systems in their original native villages which, while not always satisfying modern medical requirements, offered a good chance for survival and represented the established and accepted social and cultural attitudes of that society. It is a sad fact that these organizational and service patterns break down completely when these same people are thrown into an urbanized environment that is completely strange to them.

These results are caused by some of the well-known features of societies rapidly changing from a rural to an urbanized and industrial economy, namely high rates of population increase. Even more crucial is the explosive growth of cities;[3] new residents are forced into overcrowded apartments, shanty towns, or squatters' settlements— accommodations which need sanitary improvements much more than any other types of housing, but which lend themselves least to the provision of a workable system.

Another recurring problem has been the relentless push toward economic development regardless of long-term consequences and without always learning from the mistakes committed in the past by the industrialized countries. Thus, factories have often been improperly located, or in the haste to get them going they have been allowed to dump their discharges without any consideration of pollution problems. Natural resources have also been squandered or exploited with short-range goals in mind. For example, reckless cutting of timber or neglectful mining has resulted in unbearable water pollution through silting, or—ironic as it appears—rivers which flushed away or diluted city wastes are diverted for irrigation purposes, thus converting the river beds into open sewers.

After all, the difference between a technologically advanced area and a developing country is simply a time-lag. Consequently, sanitary solutions which would appear economically justifiable at the present but may create irreparable damage to the environment have to be stopped. This includes such precautionary measures as industrial waste control, particularly if toxic materials are involved, oil and grease removal, and, at least, careful review of the plans for all proposed new or expanded activities which are potential waste generators.

In specific instances there may be differences in the sewage composition, reflecting the dietary and sanitary habits of the people which, in turn, may call for modifications in the treatment processes. For example, the solids in sewage may consist primarily of protein or starch, depending on the dominant foodstuffs in the area; there may be very high concentration but low volume of sewage if per capita water consumption is low; household garbage may or may not be

[3] See pages 4 ff. in *Water Pollution Control,* WHO Technical Report Series No. 318 (reference 161).

disposed through sewers, thus affecting the solids' loads; and even such unusual (by Western standards) characteristics may be found as a high grit content if utensils are scoured by sand, as they are in India.

One more item which has great bearing on the problem is climate: the developing countries are mostly located in the hot and/or humid zones. The natural or artificial purification processes are affected by temperature and moisture. Consequently, careful biological and engineering design is required for each locality, since methods which perform well in the temperate climatic areas will not necessarily work equally well elsewhere. Furthermore, high temperatures can and do accelerate biochemical actions, resulting in the intensification of pollution through putrefaction, bacteriological blooms, and the growth of marine vegetation.

In outlining an approach toward sanitary planning for non-industrialized countries, we must state unequivocally that if any such country decides to adopt standards comparable to those of the economically advanced nations then, of course, all the considerations discussed in the previous chapters apply equally well, but standard methods and technology obviously must be modified in accordance with local climatological, subsoil, population density, social habit, and available construction material characteristics. However, the problems under such an approach would not be any different from those that an engineer or planner with experience in the State of Maine would encounter if he moves to Arizona, let us say. This, however, is not the usual case, and unfortunately the technical specialists sometimes find it difficult to adopt their acquired standard operating procedures to different criteria.

COLLECTION NETWORKS

Sanitation work in a city located in a developing country and experiencing all the classical symptoms mentioned above must, consequently, be geared for an intermediate level: standards as accepted in Western Europe or the United States must be reduced, but a comprehensive collection system is still required. It is to be noted that often it is assumed that the problems in these countries are the design and construction of a suitable toilet unit. These are not principal difficulties. A hole in the ground with a minimal shelter for privacy and periodic chemical disinfection is a reasonably adequate solution in a rural area. The problems only occur when the pit starts overflowing, when there are many of them too close together, when the surrounding soil becomes saturated with the effluent, and when the disinfection is not performed regularly. All this, of course, is typical of a city situation; it had been characteristic of European cities from the Middle Ages to the early twentieth century and is still found in hundreds of cities in Asia, Africa, and Latin America today.

The primary attention in an urbanized high-density area, then, must be devoted to the *removal* of domestic sewage from potential contact with the residents. It is also quite clear that the age-old practice of night soil collection by hand is unacceptable in a city because of its inherent unsanitary aspects: the containers (either the ones at the home or those used for transport) are never really clean, raw sewage even under the best of circumstances remains up to 24 hours within the home, there may be spillage along the way, odors and insects cannot be combated effectively, and it is expensive because essentially hand labor is utilized. The process can be mechanized and controlled only to a point; the disposal problem of the collected wastes is still present.[4]

A pipe system with water-borne carriage, which transports wastes away immediately after they are generated, appears at the present the only reasonable solution, since individual home disposal units are not yet developed which could be depended upon to operate with minimum supervision, no health dangers, and at rock bottom costs. A prerequisite here, of course, is the availability of a reasonably plentiful water supply within the city. Furthermore, beyond utilizing local materials and skill in construction, there is nothing in the basic design or detailed engineering of collection networks that could be modified for conditions in developing countries—a pipeline is a pipeline is a pipeline. Since these underground systems are built under minimal standards even in the industrial countries, any further short-

---

[4] See page 222 in *Metropolitan Lagos,* a special planning report prepared in 1964 by a group of technical experts for the Government of Nigeria under the sponsorship of the United Nations.

cut approach would only create a great risk of health dangers and the need for extensive maintenance in areas which can least afford it or provide it.

The area where savings can be achieved, however, is in the network layout, i.e., the density of coverage and location of inlet points. In city districts which are extremely poor, and where the family shelters are ramshackle huts, it would not be reasonable to provide connections to each temporary housing unit. A communal toilet/bathhouse is a more appropriate solution. Several advantages can be listed for such an approach:

1. The collection network may be structured in a simple system with the need for only a few lines connecting the various neighborhood toilets in a direct chain.

2. Supervision and training in the use of toilets, and bathing and washing facilities can be readily provided under such physical arrangement. This aspect may be particularly important for populations which have moved in recently from primitive rural areas.

3. The bathhouse may represent one of the few rudimentary community facilities which the government can afford to provide. It thus may form the focal point of a neighborhood and serve as its catalyst in a social sense.

The community bathhouse system, however, is not a universal answer; it is not perhaps even a permanent solution, and a few caveats must be introduced. The most important of these are the attitudes, social habits, and cultural values that certain groups of people or societies may have toward bathing and defecation, i.e., their own ideas about privacy requirements and decency. In some places communal facilities are unthinkable, and it would be presumptuous and futile to try to insist upon them. Unfortunately, this has been tried by "Western experts" in a few places. Needless to say, without success.

If community bathhouses are constructed, they can only be regarded as temporary improvements, to be replaced eventually by individual household sanitary units. Even though this may be a question of several decades, the life of the buried sewer pipes will be even longer than that. Consequently, the system built today must be designed with possible conversion in mind. The bathhouses themselves may be regarded as replaceable structures and should be built accordingly. But, since they are not likely to represent a very great capital investment, and their estimated life span is uncertain or will certainly be longer than hoped for at the time of their construction, they may as well be solid buildings. The major problem exists with respect to the pipe network, which has an extremely long life and is not easily modified once it is built underground. The logical approach here would be to regard the original pipe serving the neighborhood bathhouses as the spine from which laterals can branch off to pick up individual homes. Prefabricated sanitary cores containing all the "wet" facilities could be provided for each old or new house. This solution has been suggested by several studies.[5] It could be said that theoretically the original lines would be adequate to carry the future flow since the same number of people will be served, and the only change is that the input points are scattered instead of concentrated. Yet, this is not always a reliable conclusion; the densities will change most likely, and the per capita water consumption will certainly increase because of higher living standards and because of the convenient availability of the sanitary facilities inside a private house.

Therefore, the lines would have to be constructed originally with a greater diameter than is needed immediately. This is only a minimal cost, but one which may become more noticeable if capped house connection stubs are also incorporated. The great problem here is that this work requires a reasonably reliable master plan for the future development of the various residential sectors. The other approach would be to build new parallel collectors when conditions require them and to retain the original lines as branches or auxiliary collectors.

It is also conceivable, and probably advisable, to tie the sewer construction project to a residential upgrading program. For example, house connections for sanitary services could be offered only to those buildings which conform to certain minimum standards. The standards would have to be reasonable, within the means of the occupants, and

---

[5] Including one recently completed by the Division of Urban Planning at Columbia University for New Providence Island in the Bahamas.

achievable through cooperative efforts, or financial assistance may be required from the government within the framework of a comprehensive community improvement program. An important ancillary aspect of such work could be the legitimization of land occupancy and ownership patterns.

DISPOSAL FACILITIES

The other half of the problem is, of course, a decision with respect to treatment facilities, i.e., methods of converting the collected sewage into inert material. Since the discussion here is oriented principally toward urban conditions, usually subjected to tremendous population expansion, the first impulse—to omit treatment plants in order to save resources—will very rarely be an acceptable policy. There are bound to be squatters who will move in along the polluted river bank since these will be marginal lands avoided by everybody else who has a choice in location.

Again, there are no unique treatment methods for developing countries as distinguished from those used elsewhere. The task is rather to make a careful selection from methods available and tailor them to fit the local conditions. The basic determinant, as has been discussed previously, is the level of purity to be achieved. It is here that the local "level of tolerance" will have to be matched with available construction and maintenance funds to define a standard. Both of these elements are, in turn, a function of the treatment method used, and, therefore, considerable feedback during the decision process is involved.

In the specific selection of a treatment method or combination to achieve the desired effluent quality, several general points, beyond the obvious consideration of minimum cost, can be listed:

1. Incorporation of flexibility in design which will allow the addition of units to improve the effluent quality as standards are raised.
2. Recognition of climatic conditions; i.e., the selection of those processes which perform best in hot and humid, hot and dry, cold and humid, or other types of climates.
3. Preference given to those systems which require the least

amount of supervision and maintenance by skilled personnel, likely to be in short supply.

4. Utilizing to maximum advantage those processes which require large land acreage rather than complex mechanical equipment, since space is probably more easily available because of government ownership or relatively low costs.

In light of the above, several methods can be suggested which are among the cheapest possible approaches and are generally applicable to most climatic zones, although they will provide pollution control only at the simplest and most basic level.

The first such method would be to retain the effluent in impounding basins during low river flow and release it during periods of high volume, thus using the diluting capacity of the river as the treatment process. This system can only be accepted if the effluent volume, as compared to the river size, is relatively small, and if the periods of high flow occur at frequent and reliable intervals so as to preclude long periods of sewage storage generating septic conditions.

The next step may be sedimentation and artificial aeration in the natural drainage channels receiving the effluent. In effect, the river would be used as a treatment plant, and, while continuous energy inputs will be required, capital construction costs can be greatly minimized. Of course, that section of the river, as well as a considerable stretch downstream, will not be usable for any other purpose, and the river banks will have to be screened off from residences and other activities.

The most appropriate processes for sewage treatment in developing countries answering reasonably well all the criteria listed above and providing a most satisfactory effluent appear to be oxidation ponds and lagooning with or without artificial aeration. While they do require large amounts of land, their operation and maintenance are extremely simple, and initial construction investments are low.

The final general observation that can be made with respect to sewage treatment in developing countries is that the recovery of by-products would be of greater importance and more feasible than in the industrialized areas. This is primarily so because of the likely local scarcity of resources and availability of cheap labor. The reuse of material most probably would be at the simplest level—effluent for irrigation, sludge for fertilizer, lagoons for fish ponds, and gas for heating.[6] Such basic procedures as composting of sewage sludge and organic refuse may be of great benefit in creating often badly needed humus for near-city truck farming or other intensive agricultural uses.

While there is no doubt about the overall wisdom of a reuse policy, much specific information is still lacking to place the work on a completely rational basis. Such research would primarily involve, among other things, cost-benefit analysis of various processes and materials, considerations of toxic elements and disinfection, distribution ranges for the products, and watershed management.

HOT AND ARID ZONES. The sewage handling processes to be used in hot and arid regions must be selected recognizing that extreme water shortage is the primary problem of those zones. Consequently, year-round dilution of effluent is usually not possible, and the liquid part of sewage has to be regarded as a resource not to be thrown away.

Direct irrigation, after primary treatment or stabilization ponds, is the first suitable means of disposal,[7] provided that strict health controls are in effect. Additional problems may be the seasonal nature of agricultural water demand while sewage production proceeds at a steady rate year-round and the danger of using partially treated sewage on certain crops (e.g., aboveground vegetables) which precludes efficient crop rotation. Under a well-managed system, however, spectacular agricultural yields can be achieved.

The effluent, even partially treated, can also be used for industrial purposes, principally as a coolant. Finally, the liquid, either directly or after use in the above processes, can be returned to the ground water table through recharge wells, filter beds, or surface channels.

COLD ZONES. The difficulties experienced in sewage collection and disposal in areas with prevailing low temperatures are numerous

---

[6] The crucial need for this is indicated—admittedly an extreme case—by accusations which the Red Chinese Government made during one phase of the recent Cultural Revolution that peasants in some provinces have engaged in national sabotage through the withholding of human fertilizer.

[7] See H. I. Shuval, "Water Pollution Control in Semi-Arid and Arid Zones," in *Water Research* (reference 10), reporting on the experience in Israel.

and serious. A slowing down or even complete stoppage of bio-chemical treatment processes is possible; sedimentation also can be retarded. Yet this problem can be overcome rather easily through the construction of enclosures over process tanks, since sewage itself carries enough heat to allow the biochemical actions to take place which, in turn, generate additional heat or combustible gases. Collection pipes are exposed not so much to the risk of freezing up as they are to the thawing of the surrounding permafrost, which will cause settlement of lines and consequent cracking.

Certain purification methods, such as lagooning, need careful design and control not only because of ice formation but also because of absence of daylight during the winter or uninterrupted sunlight during the summer, both of which will interfere with the photosynthetic activity of algae. Sludge dewatering in the open air is often impractical: it will freeze in the winter and not dry fast enough in the summer because of high air humidity. Mechanical or heat drying, on the other hand, requires an energy and fuel input which is costly in most arctic areas.

Finally, odd as it may seem, potable water supply is usually a problem—surface sources freeze, wells are expensive to drill and maintain through permafrost, melting of snow requires fuel, and rainfall is not adequate in the summer. Therefore, again, the reuse of liquid discharges becomes a practical consideration.

INDIVIDUAL UNITS. The final approach to pollution control in developing countries considered here is the attempt to achieve some measure of sanitation with absolutely minimal expenditures, relying primarily on individual disposal units. It is to be emphasized that this method can only be considered for a rural area or small village where residential density is such that it permits storage and disposal or filtration through soil of sewage in the immediate proximity of a dwelling.

There is no reason why the individual disposal systems discussed previously—septic tanks—cannot be used in developing countries, except for two elements: cost and climate. A complete septic tank system is a rather expensive and elaborate improvement which will not always be in balance with the possibly crude type of housing that it is supposed to serve. The biochemical reduction process and filtration activity through the soil, which are difficult enough to control under the temperate climatic conditions for which they were designed, may be seriously upset by significantly lower or higher temperatures.

In response to these problems, a number of experiments, tests, or pilot projects have been conducted with actual improvements. This work has had two distinct areas of concern: tropical and arctic climatological zones. Various designs and operational methods have proved reasonably successful, and the descriptions of the results are available in several publications.[8] For example, in Alaska it was found that outhouses (privies) are impractical simply because of human discomfort and freezing of the wastes during winter; a chemical toilet or waste container inside the heated house presents a continuous sanitary and odor problem. Modified septic tank systems and single-house recirculation of flushing water appear to promise success, however.

SUGGESTED RESEARCH

Examination of objectives and standards under a scarce financial resources situation.

Investigation of attitudes and habits toward sanitation by various societies and cultural groups.

Analysis of treatment process performance under differing climatological conditions.

Planning study of the community-building potential of basic utility improvements.

Examination of the reuse concept under a restrictive economic situation.

[8] See references 28, 56, and 101 at end of book.

CONCLUSION

The technical knowledge to maintain a livable and clean environment is available. Treatment processes that are capable of doing the job have been developed or can be designed to do specific tasks if the needs and purposes are defined.

The major questions today are no longer related to these aspects; they are involved rather with the use of this capability. How clean an environment do we want? How much are we willing to pay for the achievement of this objective as compared to other social and economic needs? How can we achieve the greatest efficiency in doing the job?

There is little doubt that pollution levels are currently rising—more wastes are being generated on a per capita basis, there are more people and activities, and they are increasingly concentrated. These trends appear irreversible: we are not going to return to a rural culture, there will be no absolute population decreases, nor can it be expected that cities will be dispersed to any appreciable extent. The prospective mountains of waste threaten our very survival in urban centers.

Today there is less willingness on the part of the public to accept pollution as an inescapable consequence of city life; there is general awareness that this need not be so; the aspirations in all respects in all places are on the rise. These demands can be best characterized as calls for the restoration of dignity in the environment.

The long recognized detrimental effects of pollution—its social costs—such as health hazards and direct economic losses have been expanded to include odor and sight nuisances, psychological uneasiness, and impairment of recreational space. This last aspect may have extremely far-reaching consequences since, with the certainty of ever-increasing leisure time activities, no land or water area can be relegated to the barren purpose of serving as a dumping ground, particularly not near population centers. Recycling of waste materials is the solution, but it must become a national policy with all the necessary control and financial mechanisms that are currently missing.

High expenses will be involved, certainly at the beginning, and therefore a careful analysis of the reallocation of communities' resources and trade-offs in costs among a number of vital programs will be called for. There is good hope, however, that these costs will decrease as rational, large-scale systems become operative. Furthermore, the costs of not providing environmental control projects would be staggering, and, if waste management is left in the same state as it is today, the negative effects may eventually overpower completely the advantages of city life—working under the assumption that a free choice exists.

The directions toward general solutions can be indicated rather easily; their actual attainment is predicated on long and purposeful organizational work at the national, state, and local levels. The proselytizing work perhaps has been done in the United States. Now comes the stage when actual improvements must be put in effect, within a logical regional and community structure, to salvage and preserve urban living space. A large part of this responsibility for initiating and carrying out the necessary programs rests with the planning profession.

GLOSSARY

ABSORPTION (ASSIMILATIVE) CAPACITY: The natural capability of the air, water, or land environment to assimilate or dissipate measurable and limited amounts of contaminants over time through dilution, chemical and biological action, and physical processes. If this capacity is exceeded at any point, pollution will result.

ACTIVATED SLUDGE: A type of aerobic process utilized in secondary treatment plants: organic pollutants are brought in contact with biologically active micro-organisms (returned sludge) in the presence of mechanically introduced excess air.

AERATED LAGOON: An improved OXIDATION POND (*q.v.*) using mechanical aerators or diffusers. (Anaerobic action may be eliminated.)

AERATION: The artificial introduction of air into sewage, water, or effluent to create aerobic conditions and foster biochemical purification activity.

AERATOR: A device for introducing air into a liquid, either submerged (perforated pipe) or surface (mechanical paddles).

AEROBIC: A process taking place in the presence of oxygen; or a state of liquid containing free dissolved oxygen.

ANAEROBIC: A process taking place in the absence of oxygen; or a state of liquid containing no free dissolved oxygen.

BIOCHEMICAL OXIDATION: The principal purification activity by micro-organisms within an aerobic treatment process transforming organic pollutants into settleable organic or inert mineral substances.

BIOCHEMICAL OXYGEN DEMAND (B.O.D.): The amount of oxygen needed by any polluted water or sewage to allow micro-organisms to consume the suspended and dissolved biodegradable organic material found in the liquid under aerobic conditions (milligrams of oxygen per liter of liquid used up on incubation for 5 days at 20 degrees centigrade). Used as a direct indicator of pollution level measuring a deficiency.

BIODEGRADABLE: Material (usually organic) which can be reduced (digested, oxidized) by micro-organisms to form stable compounds (CO_2, water, and others).

BIOLOGICAL FILTER: *see* TRICKLING FILTER

BIOTA: The animal and plant life found within a region or an environment.

BRANCH SEWER: A sewer receiving flows from house connections and laterals.

CESSPOOL: A primitive method of sewage disposal for individual units utilizing a perforated buried tank which allows the effluent to seep into the surrounding soil but retains most of the solids.

CHEMICAL PRECIPITATION: A sewage treatment process utilizing flocs formed by chemicals as aids to sedimentation. *See also* COAGULATION

CHEMICAL TREATMENT: Sewage treatment methods utilizing various chemical processes to remove pollutants. Includes coagulation, chemical precipitation, dialysis, ion exchange, neutralization, and others.

CHLORINATION: The most commonly used final treatment step for all effluents—disinfection through the introduction of chlorine.

CHLORINE DEMAND: The amount of chlorine required by any given volume of sewage or polluted water to kill all pathogenic bacteria therein.

CLARIFICATION: The removal of settleable and floating solids from sewage.

CLARIFIER: *see* SETTLING TANK

COAGULATION: A chemical treatment process utilizing coagulating chemicals to form flocs which absorb or trap finely divided solids or colloidal particles and which are settleable.

COLIFORM BACTERIA: Nonpathogenic micro-organisms serving as indicators of bacterial contamination.

COLLECTION NETWORK: A system of sewers carrying sewage from points of generation to treatment and/or disposal facility (consisting of house connections, laterals, branch sewers, main sewers, trunk sewers, interceptors, outfall sewers, manholes, and other physical appurtenances).

COLLOIDAL PARTICLES: Material that is in a very fine state of division: particles will not settle out or pass through a semipermeable membrane.

COMBINED SEWER: A single conduit (sewer) intended for the removal of both sanitary sewage and storm water (run-off from developed areas).

COMMINUTOR: A primary treatment process combining screening with grinding of large solids, returning the shredded material to the sewage.

CONTAMINATION: A condition or state of the water environment which represents a health danger (particularly to humans) because of the presence of live pathogenic bacteria or toxic materials.

DECOMPOSITION: The separation of organic material into constituent parts or elements or into simpler compounds.

DESIGN FLOW: The hydraulic load for which a facility is designed.

DESIGN PERIOD: The time span during which proposed public works systems and improvements are to provide adequate service.

DESIGN POPULATION: The number of people to be served by proposed public works systems and improvements (the maximum number to be anticipated during the design period).

DETENTION PERIOD: The average amount of time that each unit volume of liquid is retained in a given tank or container in a flow process (detention time = tank volume divided by inflow or outflow rate).

DIALYSIS: The filtration of substances through semipermeable membranes.

DIGESTION: The conversion of organic material into simpler chemical compounds through the action of enzymes produced by living organisms.

DILUTION: A form of sewage disposal through the discharge of relatively small volumes of effluent into large receiving bodies of water thereby allowing natural purification processes to take place.

DISINFECTION: A decontamination process utilized to kill pathogenic bacteria, usually employing chlorination.

DISSOLVED MATERIAL: A substance separated in molecules and dispersed through a liquid medium.

DISSOLVED OXYGEN (D.O.): The amount of oxygen found and available for biochemical activity within a given volume of water (mg/l or ppm). The saturation point is dependent upon the temperature, chemical characteristics of the water, and barometric pressure.

DISTILLATION: A purification process involving evaporation and recondensation of vapor.

DOMESTIC SEWAGE: Wastes consisting of human bodily discharges carried by water used for flushing, soiled water from washing and laundering, and other water-borne material discarded as a by-product of regular household and human sanitary activities.

DRAINAGE BASIN: A geographic area within which all surface water flows toward one point—the lowest in elevation—from which it leaves the area.

EFFLUENT: The liquid discharged by a collection network or various treatment units of a treatment plant. Or, more generally, the liquid, solid, or gaseous product discharged or emerging from a process.

EFFLUENT CHARGE: A fixed fee levied by a regulating body against a polluter for each unit of waste discharged into public waters. The fee may be uniform for all waste producers in the area, or it may be selective according to the composition of individual wastes or the local absorption capacity. The fee may be charged continuously at all times, or it may be levied only when conditions deteriorate below a specified level.

EFFLUENT STANDARD: The maximum amount of specific pollutants allowed in discharged sewage as established by regulating agencies to achieve desirable STREAM STANDARDS (*q.v.*).

EUTROPHICATION (of a lake): The biological process whereby a water environment containing nutrients becomes gradually saturated and overwhelmed by marine vegetation and turns into a marsh.

FILTRATION: A mechanical cleaning process retaining particles within, or on top of, a porous medium; may be accompanied by biochemical action.

FLOATING SOLIDS: Suspended material in sewage which can be removed through flotation within a one-hour detention period.

FLOCCULATION: The artificial formation of flocs (loose mass of jelly-like or fibrous particles) through the addition of chemicals to sewage and mixing action.

FLOTATION: The removal of floating—lighter than water—solids utilizing settling tanks (clarifiers) with skimming devices.

FLUSHING MANHOLE: A device sometimes constructed at the up-stream end of small laterals which discharges a volume of water at intervals to remove possible sediments in sewer lines.

FORCE MAIN: A sewer flowing under pressure. Usually utilized to bring sewage from a pumping station to a manhole at a higher elevation.

GRIT REMOVAL: The removal by gravity of suspended inorganic particles (sand and grit) carried by the effluent utilizing special settling tanks within a primary treatment plant.

HOUSE (or BUILDING) CONNECTION (or SEWER): A pipe leading from the internal plumbing system of a building to a communal (or public) sewer.

IMHOFF TANK: A primary sewage treatment process combining sedimentation with anaerobic sludge digestion in one tank with no mechanical equipment.

INDIVIDUAL SEWAGE DISPOSAL: A system or process used for the removal and/or treatment of liquid wastes from a single house, building, or activity. Includes privies, cesspools, and septic tanks.

INDUSTRIAL LIQUID WASTES: Sewage generated by industrial processes and activities.

INPUT (or RAW MATERIAL) STANDARD: Regulations pertaining to materials used in production processes for the purpose of achieving acceptable EFFLUENT (*q.v.*) and STREAM (*q.v.*) STANDARDS.

INTERCEPTOR: A major sewer collecting flows from a number of main and trunk sewers and carrying the discharge to treatment or disposal facilities.

ION EXCHANGE: The separation of materials in solution by electrical charge.

LAGOONING: A simple sewage stabilization and treatment method. *See* OXIDATION POND

Or: The drying of sludge by floating it in a shallow layer over soil allowing water to evaporate or seep into the ground.

LAMPHOLE: A narrow, vertical shaft used for the insertion of a light in a sewer line between manholes for inspection purposes.

LATERAL: A minor sewer receiving flows from house connections only.

LEACHING FIELD: A system of open pipes within covered trenches allowing the effluent from a septic tank to enter the surrounding soil.

LIQUID WASTE: *see* SEWAGE

MAIN SEWER: A sewer serving as the collector for a sizable district.

MANHOLE: A vertical shaft from the surface to the sewer and used for inspection, cleaning, and repair of the system.

MICRO-ORGANISMS: Microscopic plants (bacteria, fungi, and algae) or animals (protozoa, rotifers, crustaceans, and nematodes) found in liquid wastes representing the active agents in biological treatment processes or the participants in the reduction activity.

NEUTRALIZATION: The process in which the special characteristics of two substances or solutions are destroyed.

OUTFALL SEWER: A pipe or conduit used to transport the effluent from a treatment facility to a point of final discharge (receiving body of water) or to carry raw sewage if no treatment plant is available.

OXIDATION: A chemical reaction (the loss of electrons) in which oxygen unites with other elements.

OXIDATION POND: A shallow lagoon (basin) within which waste water is purified through sedimentation and both aerobic and anaerobic biochemical action over a period.

PACKAGE PLANT: A factory-made, compact, and transportable sewage treatment facility containing all the necessary units and processes to achieve a specific effluent quality.

PATHOGENIC BACTERIA: Micro-organisms capable of producing human, animal, and plant diseases.

PERCOLATION TEST: A field test to determine the water absorption capacity of any given soil (the number of minutes required for water level inside a pit to drop one inch) prior to septic tank system design.

POLLUTANT: Any material affecting adversely the natural environment— air, water, or soil.

POLLUTER: A producer of pollutants or detrimental conditions (such as excessive heat) in the natural environment.

POLLUTION: A state under which the properties of the environment are altered in such a way as to make water, air, or soil harmful or undesirable for biological, productive, or social purposes; caused by waste discharges of excessive duration and/or concentration. *See also* WATER POLLUTION

POPULATION EQUIVALENT: The hypothetical number of people who would produce the same sewage load on treatment facilities as a given commercial or industrial activity (-ies). Conversion factors: 0.2 pounds of suspended solids/capita/day, and 0.17 or 0.2 pounds of five-day biochemical oxygen demand/capita/day.

PRIMARY TREATMENT: A series of mechanical treatment processes, including screening, skimming, and sedimentation, which remove most of the floating and suspended solids found in sewage, but which have a limited effect on colloidal and dissolved material.

PRIVY: An individual disposal system for human bodily wastes consisting usually of a cesspool under a shelter for privacy.

PUMPING STATION: An improvement consisting of a wet-well, pump, and pressure pipe (*see* FORCE MAIN), usually located underground, operated for the purpose of bringing sewage to a higher elevation.

PUTREFACTION: Decomposition of organic matter in an aerobic process giving off foul-smelling gases and incompletely oxidized products.

RIVER BASIN: *see* DRAINAGE BASIN

SAND FILTER (INTERMITTENT): A tertiary treatment process utilizing a bed of sand as a filter.

SANITARY SEWAGE: Sewage which represents a direct health and pollution hazard and includes both domestic sewage and liquid industrial wastes.

SANITARY SEWER: A sewer intended for the removal of sanitary sewage only.

SCREENING: The removal of large solids within a primary treatment plant utilizing various types of screens.

SECONDARY TREATMENT: A series of biochemical (trickling filters or activated sludge), chemical (coagulation), and/or mechanical (sedimentation) treatment processes, which remove, oxidize, or stabilize nonsettleable, colloidal, and dissolved organic materials found in sewage, following primary treatment.

SEDIMENTATION: The removal of settleable solids within primary or secondary treatment plants utilizing settling tanks which allow the pollutant particles to drop to the bottom by gravity as the sewage flows through.

SEEPAGE PIT: A buried perforated tank allowing the effluent from a septic tank to enter the surrounding soil.

SEPTIC: A biochemical state characterized by PUTREFACTION (*q.v.*).

SEPTIC TANK: A buried watertight container utilized to settle out solids, store sludge and scum, and house anaerobic (septic) biological treatment activity.

SEPTIC TANK SYSTEM: An individual sewage disposal system consisting basically of septic tank and seepage pit(s) or leaching trenches.

SETTLEABLE SOLIDS: Suspended material in sewage which can be removed through sedimentation within a one-hour detention period under the influence of gravity. (Do not include colloidal particles.)

SETTLING TANK (or CLARIFIER): The device for mechanical removal of settleable and floating solids in primary or secondary treatment plants under the influence of gravity.

SEWAGE: Liquid or water-borne wastes generated within residences, business establishments, institutions, and industrial buildings, or as by-products of any residential, commercial, industrial, social, and municipal activities.

SEWER: A conduit (usually a buried pipe) used for the collection and carrying off of sewage.

SEWER SYSTEM: The linked, man-made physical improvements intended for the collection, removal, treatment, and disposal of sewage generated within a given area; usually consisting of a collection network and a treatment facility.

SEWERAGE: The concept and general activity constituting the collection, removal, treatment, and disposal of liquid wastes.

SKIMMING: The removal of floating material from the surface of settling tanks.

SLUDGE: The concentrated slurry of pollutants removed by various treatment units from the effluent.

SLUDGE DIGESTION: A biochemical reduction process taking place within sludge digestion tanks transforming raw sludge into a relatively inert material.

SLUDGE DISPOSAL: The final step in the handling of sludge which has been removed from the effluent within a treatment plant. Includes digestion, lagooning, drying, mechanical dewatering, incineration, dumping, and burial.

SOLIDS: Pollutants, organic and inorganic, found in sewage or polluted water in a floating, suspended, or colloidal form.

SOLIDS DISPOSAL: *see* SLUDGE DISPOSAL

STABILIZATION POND: *see* OXIDATION POND: (An "oxidation pond" is the term usually used to describe a process added to a regular treatment plant for further polishing of the effluent; "stabilization pond" refers to a process which forms a treatment facility by itself.)

STORM DRAIN (or DRAIN): A sewer intended for the removal of storm water (surface run-off) only.

STREAM (or RECEIVING WATER or AMBIENT or ENVIRONMENT) STANDARD: Water quality level to be maintained in lakes and rivers as established by regulating agencies to permit specified uses of the water without hazard. *See* EFFLUENT STANDARD

SUSPENDED SOLIDS: SOLIDS (*q.v.*) that can be removed through sedimentation or filtration.

TERTIARY TREATMENT: Any sewage purification process that has the capability to remove over 98 per cent of the pollutants from sewage, following a secondary treatment plant.

TOXIC: Capable, through chemical action, of killing, injuring, or impairing an organism.

TREATMENT: The artificial removal of pollutants from sewage and/or their transformation into an inert state and/or the altering of the objectionable constituents by controlled physical, chemical, and/or biological processes.

TREATMENT PLANT: A contiguous system of processes and units designed and used for the removal of pollutants from sewage.

TRICKLING FILTER: A type of aerobic process utilized in secondary treatment plants: effluent is sprinkled over coarse filtration material covered by active biological growths which interact with organic pollutants.

TRUNK SEWER: A major sewer collecting flows from a large area.

TURBIDITY: Visible pollution due to suspended material in water causing a reduction in light transmission ability.

WASTE CONTROL: A term that includes, in addition to physical collection and treatment, actions related to waste generation and their release from establishments through public regulations.

WASTE DISPOSAL: A somewhat obsolete and imprecise term used to describe the standard methods of waste collection, removal, and often treatment. The problem is that very little is really disposed: the wastes are transported away from human settlements and, at best, changed to a less noxious material.

WASTE MANAGEMENT: The currently emerging term describing a comprehensive and rational systems approach toward environmental quality where the desirable objectives suggest and dictate control measures. It includes all the coordinated actions (usually by public agencies) designed to achieve greatest efficiency in the control of all wastes for a community or a region: setting of policy, determination of environmental standards, enforcement of regulations, collection and treatment of wastes, and monitoring of air, water, and soil quality.

WASTES: The unwanted and economically unusable by-products at a given location and time of any production or consumption activity. It is to be noted that these by-products may have a use at another place and time in perhaps a modified form. The wastes occur in three physical states and very often can be transformed from one into another: solid, liquid, and gaseous.

WATER POLLUTION: A condition or state of the water environment under which the usefulness of the water is impaired or eliminated for domestic, industrial, and recreational purposes; aquatic biota suffers or is destroyed; and offensive and unnatural sights, smells, and tastes are present.

WATERSHED: A DRAINAGE BASIN (*q.v.*). Also an area from which a community receives its water.

ZIMMERMAN PROCESS: A patented sewage treatment process achieving oxidation of organic material in a closed container under high pressure and temperature.

APPENDICES

A. SEWAGE GENERATION RATES FOR COMMERCIAL AND PUBLIC ESTABLISHMENTS

	Gallons per person per day
Hotels	50 to 150
Motels (per bed space)	50 to 125
Restaurants (toilet and kitchen wastes per patron)	7 to 10
Additional for bars and cocktail lounges	2
Tourist courts with individual bath units	50 to 120
Luxury camps	100 to 150
Camps	25 to 40
Day camps (no meals)	15
Day schools (with cafeterias, showers)	15 to 25
Boarding schools	75 to 100
Day workers at schools or offices	12 to 35
Hospitals	150 to 250 or more
Other institutions	75 to 125
Factory workers (per shift)	15 to 35
Picnic parks (with bathhouses and showers)	10
Swimming pools and bathhouses	10
Drive-in theaters (per car space)	5 to 10
Theaters (per seat)	5
Places of assembly	3 to 10
Airports (per passenger)	3 to 5
Self-service laundries (per wash)	50
Stores (per toilet room)	400
Service stations (per vehicle served)	10

APPENDIX A (continued)

	Gallons per day per 1,000 sq. ft.
Hotels	600 to 1,100
Office buildings	100 to 500
Department stores	100 to 400
Apartment hotels	200 to 400
	Gallons per day per acre
Light industry	14,000
Hotels, stores, and office buildings	60,000
Markets, warehouses, wholesale establishments	15,000
High-cost residential	7,500
Medium-cost residential	8,000
Low-cost residential	16,000

SOURCES:
  USPHS, *Manual of Septic Tank Practice*
  Seelye, E. E., *Design*
  Design and Construction of Sanitary and Storm Sewers (WPCF Manual No. 9)
  Public Works Magazine

B. EFFICIENCIES OF
SEWAGE TREATMENT UNITS

	Per cent removal of		
	B.O.D.	Suspended solids	B. coliform
Fine screening	5–10	2–20	10–20
Plain sedimentation	25–40	40–70	25–75
Plain aeration and final settling	60–70		
Chemical precipitation	50–85	70–90	40–80
High-rate trickling filtration (with pre- and post-sedimentation)	65–95	65–92	80–95
Low-rate trickling filtration (with pre- and post-sedimentation)	70–95	70–92	90–95
High-rate activated sludge treatment (with pre- and post-sedimentation)	65–95	65–95	80–95
Conventional activated sludge treatment (with pre- and post-sedimentation)	75–95	85–95	95–98
Intermittent sand filtration	90–95	85–95	95–98
Various tertiary processes	98–99	99	—
Package plants	75–90		
Chlorination of raw or settled sewage	15–30	—	90–95
Chlorination of biologically treated sewage	—	—	98–99

SOURCES:
  Seelye, E. E., *Design*, p. 19–01
  Abbett, R. W., *American Civil Engineering Practice*
  Salvato, J. A., *Environmental Sanitation*, p. 262

C. FRESH WATER TOLERANCE LIMITS FOR VARIOUS USES

Quality Indicators	Units of Measurement	Raw Municipal Water	Recreation (body contact)	Tolerant Fish and Aquatic Life	Intolerant Fish and Aquatic Life	Livestock and Wildlife	Irrigation	Industrial Cooling Water	Esthetics
Maximum temperature	°F	95	95	93	75	95	95	95	
Coliform bacteria	nmbr./100ml	5,000	1,000	—	—	—			
Streptococci	nmbr./100ml	100	100						
Dissolved oxygen (min)	mg/l	some		4	6	some	some	some	some
Acidity range	pH	5–9	5–9	6–9	6–9	5–9	5–9	5–9	n.a.
Phenolics	mg/l	0.05	0.2	0.2	0.2	n.a.	n.a.	n.a.	0.2
Chloride ions	mg/l	250	n.a.	—	—	1,500	150 or more	n.a.	n.a.
Ammonia nitrogen	mg/l	n.a.	n.a.	1.5	0.4	5,000	beneficial	n.a.	n.a.
Dissolved solids	mg/l	500	n.a.	10,000	5,000	7,000	1,000 to 3,000	—	n.a.
Phosphates	mg/l	0.4	n.a.	small amounts are beneficial		n.a.	beneficial	beneficial	—
Cyanides	mg/l	0.2	0.2	0.05	0.025	0.2	—	n.a.	n.a.
Fluorides	mg/l	0.8 to 1.7	n.a.	1.5	1.5	0.8 to 1.7	10	n.a.	n.a.
Odor									
Oil									
Floating solids									
Bottom deposits	} not to be substantially visible or noticeable								
Turbidity									
Color									

SOURCE: *Water Quality Criteria* by Engineering and Technical Research Committee, American Petroleum Institute, 1967
n.a. = not applicable.

D. TREATMENT PLANT CONSTRUCTION COSTS

Population Size	Construction Costs per Capita			
	Stabilization Ponds	Primary Treatment (separate sludge digestion)	Activated Sludge*	Trickling Filters* (separate sludge digestion)
100	$36			
500	20	$70	$85	$100
1,000	16	56	65	80
5,000	9	35	40	45
10,000	7	27	29	30
50,000	4	17	18	14
100,000		13	13	11
coefficient of correlation (r)	0.54	0.66	−0.74	−0.74

* Population equivalents used

SOURCE:
USPHS, *Modern Sewage Treatment Plants: How Much Do They Cost?* 1964

E. GENERAL CRITERIA FOR SEWAGE COLLECTION NETWORKS

HOUSE CONNECTIONS

Minimum diameter: 4 inches

Preferred diameter: 6 inches or more

Slope: ¼ inch/foot

Connection to lateral: Preferably entering at the upper portion of the lateral with a Y in the direction of flow.

The maintenance of each house connection is the responsibility of the property owner.

NETWORK STRUCTURE

Public sewers are located in street rights-of-way; usually along the center line. If they can be placed under unpaved sections, repair and excavation costs can be minimized.

Location in separate easements may be required to achieve an efficient flow configuration, to reach isolated properties, or to cope with restraining topographic conditions. Easements are to be avoided because of maintenance and administrative complications and possible cost increases.

Access to all properties must be provided, within a general least-cost restraint—usually achieved with a system of minimum aggregate length of pipes and fewest special improvements (such as pumping stations, siphons, or high-strength lines). Maximum physical separation should be provided between sewer lines and water mains: to be placed whenever possible on opposite sides of the street and at different elevations at points where they cross.

The network pattern should take a tree-like or natural tributary watercourse arrangement allowing free gravity flow down existing slopes into progressively larger conduits.

The topmost points are on dead-end branches located to allow entry by a house connection from the last (highest) property to be serviced.

The system should lead directly by gravity flow to a treatment plant. If low points are encountered which prevent continuous free flow or which can be drained only by sewers in excessively deep trenches, pumping stations and force mains may be provided to lift flows to higher conduits from where gravity flow can be continued.

Minimum velocity: 2 feet/second to maintain self-cleaning flow. (Flushing manholes may be added.)

Maximum velocity: 10 feet/second to avoid excessive abrasive effect.

Sewage flow velocity is a function of the slope, diameter, and interior surface characteristics (smoothness) of the pipe and flow volume (quantity). Detailed pipe design involves the hydraulic calculation and balancing of all of these factors to achieve a satisfactory combination: enough capacity, minimum depth trench, and flow within the allowable velocity range.

Manhole location: at the end of lines, at the junction of lines, at all changes in pipe diameter and horizontal and vertical alignment, and not farther apart under any conditions than 300 feet. (The last requirement may be 400 or 500 feet if the locality has appropriate cleaning devices to reach that distance; for pipes which are large enough to allow the entry of maintenance men, the distances may be even longer.)

In conventional sewer design all pipe sections between manholes must be straight to allow visual inspection and rodding through. With modern cleaning equipment, curved alignment may be permitted.

The change in direction of flow at any one manhole should not exceed 90°.

Minimum pipe diameter: 8 inches.

Depth of pipe: Pipe must be below frost line (4 to 6 feet in northern United States) with adequate cover to cushion traffic loads (ordinarily 2 feet or more) and must be able to drain the basements of the properties served (3 feet below basement floor). For very deep basements and under unusual conditions, individual sewage ejectors can be installed.

Deep trenches which require shoring during construction or must be cut in hard material increase costs greatly.

Minimum pipe slopes which would be universally applicable cannot be specified. A calculation of the linked factors in each case is required, but usually a 0.33 to 0.5 per cent grade for small sewers and 0.15 to 0.25 per cent for large are limiting values.

A pipe slope parallel to ground slope (constant trench depth) will usually be the most economical solution.

ANNOTATED BIBLIOGRAPHY

Of the literally thousands of references which have been published during the last decade in the liquid waste field and of the 500 sources which were read in connection with this project, the following list of over 160 items includes those which were judged to contain information useful to the planner and other professionals involved in water quality and environmental control. Highly technical and specialized publications have been omitted, as well as some very good but obscure sources not easily available. Likewise, a number of very detailed references quoted in the preceding text are excluded from the general bibliography.

The backbone of the list is a number of sanitary engineering and public health textbooks and references chosen from the many currently in print. These, of course, contain much information exceeding the needs of the urban planner, but, since there are no such works directly suitable for the planner, there is no alternative but to start with these sources.

In the areas of administration and financing, only those publications which refer specifically to water pollution problems are included, but many of these analyze this aspect within a much broader context.

An effort was made to exclude small articles, but, in order to obtain a reasonably comprehensive coverage, in many subjects—advanced treatment methods, water reuse, suburban problems, planning considerations—for which full-scale books are not yet written, they had to be listed.

A representative selection of sources from foreign countries is also included. These are important because they illustrate European and Latin American experiences which are not always adequately reported in the American sources, they provide foreign-language terminology and, with respect to developing countries, often give examples which relate to the countries using the respective languages (former colonies). There are many good books published in Britain and Germany; the French sources are more scarce; Spanish-speaking countries rely primarily on translations from English; and the Russian references hide behind a language barrier.

As will be apparent from a quick scanning of the bibliography, many items on specific topics come from a few sources: United States governmental agencies (particularly the Public Health Service), the World Health Organization, and articles published in the *Journal of the Water Pollution Control Federation.*

As is customary, a list of twelve—an arbitrary number—"most basic" references has been selected, and these items are marked with an asterisk (*).

For further research into more detailed aspects of the water sanitation problem, a great wealth of information exists, and some suggestions for retrieval can be given.

A number of bibliographies have been published on specific aspects of environmental control by various agencies. These include several series by the U.S. Public Health Service, the *American Journal of Public Health,* the *Journal of the WPCF* (as an annual feature), the Institute for Community Development of Michigan State University, U.S. Department of the Interior (Office of Water Resources Research), Texas Water Development Board, and a number of others.

Another group of references that represents a great reservoir of material is the records of Congressional hearings conducted in connection with proposed bills in pollution control during the last decade. Unfortunately, however, this information is not in a readily usable or even organized form. One is almost required to read all the transcripts in their entirety to find the desired data. Several hearings have taken a very comprehensive view, and even national surveys of water pollution, its control and abatement have been done under the auspices of the U.S. Congress.

Somewhat similar conditions exist with respect to conference proceedings. Extensive meetings at which many papers on the subject of wastes were presented have been held by the American Medical Association, American Society of Civil Engineers, American Public Works Association, U.S. Public Health Service, National Academy of Sciences, Water Pollution Control Federation, and others, including foreign organizations. Experts have also met under the sponsorship of various educational institutions such as the universities of Florida, Kansas, Michigan, Pittsburgh, North Carolina, Duke, Vanderbilt, Manhattan College, King's College (Newcastle, Britain), and others.

The annual indices of several technical magazines and the Engineering Index will also lead to useful references for specific purposes. The major magazines in the water pollution control area are, again, the *Journal of the WPCF, Public Works, American Water Works Association Journal, The Journal of the Sanitary Engineering Division* of ASCE and its annual *Proceedings, Civil Engineering, Congressional Record, Water and Pollution Control, Water Works and Wastes Engineering, Water and Sewage Works, American City, Air and Water Pollution* (Britain), *Canadian Municipal Utilities, Engineer* (Britain), *Gesundheits-Ingenieur* (Germany), *Travaux* (France), *Saneamiento* (Argentina).

Generally speaking, articles and reports referring exclusively to specific localities and their problems have also been excluded from this bibliography. However, very often such sources offer useful information, particularly procedural methodology, specific findings, and standards— many of them can be found listed in the American Society of Planning Officials *Newsletter*'s "Planner's Library" appearing regularly or in *Metropolitan Surveys,* published annually by the Graduate School of Public Affairs, State University of New York at Albany.

Finally, the publications of various trade associations and manufacturers of equipment used in sewage works (such as Certain-Teed Products Corporation, Clay Sewer Pipe Association, National Lime Association, In-Sink-Erator, Portland Cement Association, and others) can be suggested. Care in selection, however, is recommended since some of them are serious investigations; others explain pollution and its control as preludes to a sales pitch for their own products. They usually can be obtained free of charge.

REFERENCES

1. Advisory Commission on Intergovernmental Relations. *Intergovernmental Responsibilities for Water Supply and Sewage Disposal in Metropolitan Areas.* Washington, D.C.: 1962, 135 pp.

   A publication discussing the planning, policy making, operating, and regulatory roles of all three levels of government and making recommendations which stress the metropolitan area as the primary planning unit, asking for greater financial investment in facilities, better enforcement of ordinances and, above all, speaking out against any fragmentation of responsibilities.

2. Advisory Commission on Intergovernmental Relations. *Performance of Urban Functions—Local and Areawide.* Washington, D.C.: September 1963, Number M21 (rev.), 281 pp.

   The work presents information which is largely derivative but thorough in the analysis of methods available to various levels of government in guarding the quality of the environment.

3. Agricultural Research Service, U.S. Department of Agriculture. *Farmstead Sewage and Refuse Disposal.* Washington, D.C.: 1963, Agricultural Information Bulletin, Number 274, 25 pp.

   A practical evaluation of individual waste disposal systems which discusses rural sewerage and the various methods available for disposal, including privies.

4. American Public Health Assoc., et al. *Standard Methods for the Examination of Water and Wastewater.* New York: APHA, Inc., 1960, 626 pp.

   A manual of procedures to measure pollution levels.

5. Anderson, R. T. *Comprehensive Planning for Environmental*

Health. Ithaca, N.Y.: Center for Housing and Environmental Studies, Cornell University: 1962, Misc. Papers Number 2, 203 pp.

A Master's thesis discussing environmental problems as related to planning work; one of the first such attempts and somewhat general in nature.

6. Babbitt, H. E., and E. R. Baumann. *Sewerage and Sewage Treatment.* New York: John Wiley, 1958, 790 pp.

A standard engineering textbook, among the most complete ones, devoted exclusively to sewerage, containing comparisons of treatment processes, analyses of new methods, operational guidelines, and even descriptions of small systems.

7. *Background on Water Pollution: A Manual for Municipal, State and Federal Planners.* New York: National Water Institute; Water and Wastewater Equipment Mfrs. Association, n.d., 22 pp.

A brief but comprehensive survey of all aspects of sewerage; for the non-technician.

8. Baxter, S. S. "Economic Considerations of Water Pollution Control." *Journal WPCF,* Vol. 37, No. 10 (October 1965), pp. 1363–69.

A discussion of cost-benefit methods in reference to the water environment and its waste assimilation capacity.

9. Bregman, J. I., and S. Lenormand. *The Pollution Paradox.* New York: Spartan Books, 1966, 191 pp.

The book, a joint effort by a physicist and a journalist, offers a wealth of well-analyzed data, without losing readability, on both water and air pollution. Solutions and action programs are suggested.

10. Brown, R. M. "Urban Planning for Environmental Health." *Public Health Reports,* Vol. 79, No. 3 (March 1964), pp. 201–04.

A review of the fringe area problems under intensifying development.

11. Building Research Advisory Board. *Residential Building Sewers.* Washington, D.C.: National Academy of Sciences, National Research Council, 1960, Bulletin No. 787, 126 pp.

A detailed investigation for FHA of the materials used for pipelines.

12. Canham, R. A. "Status of Federal Water Pollution Control Legislation." *Journal WPCF,* Vol. 38, No. 1 (January 1966), pp. 1–8.

A review of Federal legislation in effect, particularly the Water Quality Act of 1965, with a look into the future.

13. Carr, D. E. *Death of the Sweet Waters.* New York: W. W. Norton and Co., 1966, 257 pp.

The book, intended for the popular market, contains technical information and is thoroughly documented. The author is a practicing chemist and environmental expert whose primary concern is an adequate water supply.

14. Castel, E. N. "Economics of Water Pollution Control." *Journal WPCF,* Vol. 38, No. 5 (May 1966), pp. 789–93.

    A general survey of the economic approach in river basin quality management.

15. Cillie, G. C., et al. "The Reclamation of Sewage Effluents for Domestic Use." *Journal WPCF,* Vol. 38, No. 3 (March 1966), pp. 341–42.

    A report on the experience in Windhoek, South West Africa.

16. Clark, J. W., and W. Viessman, Jr. *Water Supply and Pollution Control.* Scranton: International Textbook Co., 1965, 575 pp.

    A standard engineering textbook handling both aspects of water use at an advanced mathematical and technical level, including recent process developments and water reuse.

17. Committee on Fringe Area Sanitation Problems, APHA. "Fringe Area Sanitation." *Public Health Reports,* Vol. 76, No. 4 (April 1961), pp. 309–14.

    A description as to what happens and what needs to be done in general sanitation when rural areas become developed; recommendations for action.

*18. Committee on Pollution, NAS. *Waste Management and Control: A Report to the Federal Council for Science and Technology.* Washington, D.C.: National Academy of Sciences, National Research Board, Publication No. 1400, 1966, 257 pp.

    The work, currently emerging as the definitive survey of pollution and its implications, approaches the subject as an underlying condition and effect of contemporary urban life, not from the viewpoint of any one discipline. Various chapters of the book define the pollution problem, discuss the areas where our knowledge, legal means, or organizational patterns fall short, and propose solutions, generally and specifically. A very extensive technical section (appendix) ranges over the soil, water, and air environments and types of pollutants and their control.

19. Coulter, J. B. "What Is a Comprehensive Water Pollution Control Program?" *Journal WPCF,* Vol. 38, No. 6 (June 1966), pp. 1011–22.

    A thorough discussion of the principal steps and actors involved in the development of a comprehensive water pollution control program. The sequence ranges from information gathering and analysis to the evaluation of results.

20. "The Crisis in Water: Its Sources, Pollution and Depletion." Special issue of *Saturday Review* (October 23, 1965), pp. 23–80.

A series of articles on the causes of water shortage and pollution with descriptions of the situation in Chicago, Cleveland, Los Angeles, Miami, New York, Phoenix, Seattle, and St. Louis.

21. Culp, R. L., and R. E. Roderick. "The Lake Tahoe Water Reclamation Plant." *Journal WPCF,* Vol. 38, No. 2 (February 1966), pp. 147–55.

A discussion of the experience with high-purity sewage treatment at Lake Tahoe.

22. Daley, R. *The World Beneath the City.* Philadelphia: J. B. Lippincott, 1959, 233 pp.

A book with pure entertainment value that nevertheless may provide some insights—literally and figuratively—into the buried and invisible utilities, as found in New York City.

23. Del Duca, M. G., and J. M. Fuscoe. "Application of Advances in Space Technology to Water Resources Management." *Journal WPCF,* Vol. 38, No. 6 (June 1966), pp. 976–89.

Well-documented proposals as to how the regenerative closed-cycle idea can be applied to river basin management through the use of systems analysis and other advanced technologies.

24. Demidow, L. G., and G. G. Schigorin. *Kanalisation,* 2 volumes. Leipzig: Fachbuchverlag GMBH, 1953 and 1955, 349 and 332 pp.

The book, a translation from Russian into German, is a complete treatise on sewage collection and disposal with many drawings and large plans. While the differences between the American and European methods and equipment are not particularly great, one can observe a number of interesting and unfamiliar approaches in the Russian practice.

25. Domke, H. R. "Public Health in the Metropolitan Setting." *Public Health Reports,* Vol. 77, No. 5 (May 1962), pp. 383–87.

A general discussion of metropolitan life and the pressures on human, physical, and psychic health.

26. Dubosch, Ch. *Egouts Publics: Epuration.* Bruxelles: Editions G.I.G., 1951, 368 pp.

A review and discussion of a great variety of treatment processes, ranging from very simple to complex ones.

27. Dunbar, D. D., and J. G. F. Henry. "Pollution Control Measures for Stormwater and Combined Sewer Overflows." *Journal WPCF,* Vol. 38, No. 1 (January 1966), pp. 9–26.

A report on the pollution created by overflows, with suggested solutions.

28. Duncan, D. L. "Individual Household Recirculating Waste Dis-

posal System for Rural Alaska." *Journal WPCF,* Vol. 36, No. 12 (December 1964), pp. 1468–78.

A discussion of the experience with two pilot systems in cold regions.

29. Ehlers, V. M., and E. W. Steel. *Municipal and Rural Sanitation.* New York: McGraw-Hill, 1965, 643 pp.

One of several competent public health references which discusses municipal and individual water supply and sewage disposal systems, food protection, refuse disposal, and other sanitation topics. A detailed description of public health organizations and some planning considerations are distinguishing additional features of this work.

30. Eliassen, R., and B. C. McBeath. "Sensitivity Analysis of Activated Sludge Economics." *Journal of the Sanitary Engineering Division, ASCE Proceedings,* Vol. 92, No. SA 2 (April 1966), pp. 147–67.

A theoretical study attempting to optimize the performance of a specific plant through a change of input variables.

31. Engineering Science, Inc. *Feasibility of Curved Alignment for Residential Sanitary Sewers.* Washington, D.C.: FHA Technical Studies Program, June 1959, 200 pp.

A detailed analysis of a specific, unconventional aspect of sewer design; with examples.

*32. Environmental Pollution Panel, President's Science Advisory Committee. *Restoring the Quality of Our Environment.* Washington, D.C.: The White House, November 1965, 317 pp.

Similar coverage of material as in *Waste Management and Control,* but there is little duplication between the two works, and they complement each other. The stress in this one is on direct recommendations for action by the Federal Government.

33. Escritt, L. B. *Sewerage and Sewage Disposal: Calculations, Design and Specifications.* London: C. R. Books, Ltd., 1965, 488 pp.

A general sanitation textbook from Britain containing a number of interesting items for the planner, such as a complete discussion of the layout of lines and sample specifications. Its most useful part is the description of European practice in liquid waste disposal.

*34. Fair, G. M., J. C. Geyer, and D. A. Okun. *Water and Wastewater Engineering.* Volume I: *Water Supply and Waste Water Removal,* 1966; Volume II: *Water Purification and Waste Water Treatment,* 1968. New York: John Wiley.

This significant book contains all the technical data required in an engineering text, but it also incorporates such items as detailed methods of information analysis and optimization techniques. Especially noteworthy features are the close linkage of water supply and sewage disposal showing interdependence and the somewhat hesitant but nevertheless important attempts to include some discussion of city and regional planning implications.

35. Federal Housing Administration. *Minimum Design Standards for Community Sewerage Systems.* Washington, D.C.: July 1963, FHA Bulletin No. 720, 65 pp.

The manual provides a complete range of specifications for collection systems and treatment facilities serving properties offered as security for mortgage insurance.

36. Federal Housing Administration. *Ownership and Organization of Central Water and Sewage Systems.* Washington, D.C.: 1964, FHA Bulletin No. 1300, 18 pp.

The publication concentrates on the problems faced by developers of housing projects in providing utility service and discusses acceptable methods, primarily property owners' associations and trust deeds.

37. Federal Water Pollution Control Administration. *Focus on Clean Water: An Action Program for Community Organizations.* Washington, D.C.: Publication No. WP–7, 1966, 31 pp.

A publication aimed at citizens' groups and taxpayers, providing information as to how local action programs can be initiated and guided forward.

38. "The Fouling of the American Environment." Special issue of *Saturday Review.* (May 22, 1965), pp. 31–98.

A series of articles on environmental problems in the United States, primarily air pollution, with a number of case studies.

39. Frieden, B. J. *Metropolitan America: Challenge to Federalism (Commission Findings and Proposals).* Washington, D.C.: Advisory Commission on Intergovernmental Relations, Publication M–31, 1966, 176 pp.

Chapter III offers a thorough analysis of the administrative problems encountered in the provision of water and removal of wastes under a metropolitan situation with three participating levels of government.

40. Fringe Area Sanitation Practices Committee, APHA. "Environmental Health in Community Growth." *American Journal of Public Health,* Vol. 53, No. 5 (May 1963), pp. 802–22.

A general reference for government officials, public health workers, consultants, and others involved in sanitary planning, which outlines areas for action in legislation, planning, finance, and community participation and describes the problems created by community growth.

41. Furman, R. de S., et al. *Sewerage Planning.* Gainesville, Fla.: University of Florida, 1956, Florida Engineering Series No. 2, 86 pp.

The work offers brief chapters on many aspects of liquid waste disposal: from history of treatment systems to the responsibilities of the engineer, the contractor, and the community. Financing and suburban systems are also covered in language understandable to the layman.

42. Geyer, J. C., and J. J. Lentz. "An Evaluation of the Problems of Sewer System Design." *Journal WPCF,* Vol. 38, No. 7 (July 1966), pp. 1138–47.

A report on a study of problems encountered in a number of cities including per capita flow rates, infiltration, and causes of stoppage.

43. Goldman, M. I. (edit.). *Controlling Pollution: The Economics of a Cleaner America.* Englewood Cliffs, N.J.: Prentice-Hall, 1967, 175 pp.

The book, despite its misleading title (there is very little on specific economics in the book) and several inferior presentations, contains a number of good articles on the dimensions of the pollution problem and its social implications. Several major case studies from this country and abroad are very useful.

44. Goodman, A. S., and W. E. Dobbins. "Mathematical Model for Water Pollution Control Studies." *Journal of the Sanitary Engineering Division, ASCE Proceedings,* Vol. 92, No. SA 6 (December 1966), 19 pp.

A theoretical approach to an optimization system for an entire river basin studying the interrelationships of water pollution programs with population, industry, water supply, recreation, etc.

45. Gordon, M. *Sick Cities: Psychology and Pathology of American Urban Life.* New York: The Macmillan Co., 1963, 366 pp.

An indictment of city ills—bacteriological and psychological—that includes also chapters on the water problem.

*46. Gotaas, H. B., et al. "Frontiers in Wastewater Management: Technological, Financial, Administrative." *Journal WPCF,* Vol. 38, No. 5 (May 1966), pp. 745–73.

A major article calling for modern management methods in pollution control and for judicious planning in the use of scarce resources toward defined social and economic goals. A plea is made for the assignment of appropriate responsibilities—functional and financial—at the various levels of government; the observation is also made that present programs are not adequate. Effluent charges, the use of large-scale pollution control facilities, problems of costs and benefits with respect to public health, esthetics, recreation, and the entire question of planning and management of river basins are considered.

47. Graham, F., Jr. *Disaster by Default: Politics and Water Pollution,* Philadelphia: J. B. Lippincott, 1966, 256 pp.

The book is in the grand tradition of American muckraking journalism. The concern of the author is convincing in his description of a number of shameful water pollution occurrences; the main attack is against irresponsible industrialists, although lethargic or incompetent (or worse) politicians do not escape either.

48. Gray, D. C. "Financing Sewerage Facilities." *Journal WPCF,* Vol. 35, No. 1 (January 1963), pp. 69–74.

An examination of the conventional means—primarily municipal bonds—used in financing sanitary improvements.

49. Green, R. S., et al. "Data Handling Systems in Water Pollution Control." *Journal of the Sanitary Engineering Division, ASCE Proceedings,* Vol. 92, No. SA 1 (February 1966), pp. 55–67.

A work proposing a mathematical predictive model with monitoring stations which can forecast impending conditions in terms of pollution levels and suggest, or even effectuate, corrective and preventive actions for an entire river basin.

50. Guerrée, H. *Pratique de L'assainissement des Agglomérations.* Paris: Editions Eyrolles, 1961, 219 pp.

A general text at a somewhat elementary level, drawing from the experience in French-speaking countries.

51. Gurnham, C. F. *Industrial Wastewater Control.* New York: Academic Press, 1965, 476 pp.

A technical source on industrial liquid waste control methods for specific manufacturing processes.

52. Hammond, R. J. *Benefit-cost Analysis and Water Pollution Control.* Stanford, Calif.: Food Research Institute, Stanford University, 1960, 95 pp.

An early publication which attempts to establish the framework and examines the feasibility of cost-benefit analysis recognizing the problems that stand in the way of immediate application of the method.

53. Hardenbergh, W. A., and E. B. Rodie. *Water Supply and Waste Disposal.* Scranton, Pa.: International Textbook Co., 1961, 503 pp.

A general text, but it includes some standards with an outline of design procedures and check lists of items not found elsewhere.

54. Herber, L. *Crisis in Our Cities.* Englewood Cliffs, N.J.: Prentice-Hall, 1965, 239 pp.

A discussion of serious physical problems facing urban residents: air and water pollution, overcrowding, congestion, and psychic pressures.

55. Herfindahl, O. C., and A. V. Kneese. *Quality of the Environment: An Economic Approach to Some Problems in Using Land, Water, and Air.* Washington, D.C.: Resources for the Future, Inc., The Johns Hopkins Press, 1965, 96 pp.

The study deals with environment in its broadest sense and also incorporates a general investigation of water pollution with a plea for a regional approach. Suggestions toward future research and action programs are made.

56. Hickey, J. L. S., and D. L. Duncan. "Performance of Single Family Septic Tank Systems in Alaska." *Journal WPCF,* Vol. 38, No. 8 (August 1966), pp. 1298–1309.

An evaluation of septic tanks in the Anchorage and Fairbanks area.

57. Hirsch, L. "Package Plants Provide Sewerage for a Fast Growing Community." *Public Works,* Vol. 92, No. 2 (February 1961), pp. 111–13.

An article on the experience in Madison Township, New Jersey.

58. Hopkins, E. S., and W. H. Schulze. *The Practice of Sanitation.* Baltimore: The Williams and Wilkins Co., 1958, 487 pp.

A standard public health textbook starting with food protection but containing also good chapters on rural and urban sewage disposal, stream pollution, industrial wastes, and housing sanitation.

59. Institute of Public Administration. *Industrial Incentives for Water Pollution Abatement.* Washington, D.C.: U.S. Public Health Service, February 1965, 95 pp.

A discussion of the problems in obtaining manufacturers' compliance with antipollution regulations.

60. Irrigation and Drainage Division, ASCE. Conference Papers, *Development of the Total Watershed.* New York: ASCE, 1966, 400 pp.

A collection of papers that includes examinations of the use of wastewater for irrigation and ground water recharge, as well as general pollution problems.

61. Isaac, P. C. G. *Public Health Engineering.* London: Spon, 1953, 277 pp.

A general sanitation textbook that covers the public health field and includes not only water supply and sewage disposal, but also aspects of river pollution, industrial wastes, refuse disposal, air pollution, and even district heating in terms of European experience.

62. Jacobs, H. L., et al. "Water Quality Criteria: Stream vs. Effluent Standards." *Journal WPCF,* Vol. 37, No. 3 (March 1965), pp. 292–315.

A composite article that outlines the pollution problem, suggests general guidelines, describes methods of measurement, and discusses criteria. Also presents the views of industry and conservationists.

63. James, G. V. "Domestic Sewage," in *Water Treatment.* London: The Technical Press, Ltd., 1965, pp. 247–96.

This section (Part 3) concentrates on a number of specific biological treatment processes, some not often found or utilized in the United States.

64. Jarrett, H. (edit.). *Environmental Quality in a Growing Economy.* Washington, D.C.: Resources for the Future, Inc., The Johns Hopkins Press, 1966, 173 pp.

A collection of essays dealing with the economics of environment, goals, public attitudes, and administrative machinery.

65. Joint Committee of the ASCE and WPCF. *Sewage Treatment Plant Design.* New York: ASCE, 1959, Manual of Engineering Practice No. 36, 375 pp.

Precise, technical design information with detailed descriptions of all pieces of equipment, apparatus, operating procedures, and construction methods of sewage plants.

66. Joint Committee of the WPCF and ASCE. *Design and Construction of Sanitary and Storm Sewers.* WPCF Manual of Practice No. 9, ASCE Manual of Engineering Practice No. 37, 1960, 283 pp.

Companion volume to the previous work dealing with all aspects of sewer network design and construction, including hydraulics and building methods. This work, unfortunately, lacks even a single drawing of a typical layout, but is strong in the details of system elements.

67. Kaiser, C. B., Jr. "Organization of a Metropolitan Sewer District." *Journal WPCF,* Vol. 38, No. 4 (April 1966), pp. 555–61; and "Administrative and Financial Aspects of Operating a Metropolitan Sewer District." *Journal WPCF,* Vol. 39, No. 4 (April 1967), pp. 501–17.

The articles describe the problems in organizing metropolitan sewer districts through the case study of St. Louis.

68. Keefer, C. E. "Tertiary Sewage Treatment." *Public Works,* Vol. 93, Nos. 11 and 12 (November and December 1962), pp. 109–12 and 81–83.

A two-part article discussing conditions where high-level treatment is needed and describing processes in use in United States and abroad.

69. Kerri, K. D. "A Dynamic Model for Water Quality Control." *Journal WPCF*, Vol. 39, No. 5 (May 1967), pp. 772–86.

A proposed model based on the formation of a cooperative association with cost allocations.

70. Kindsvater, C. E. (edit.). *Organization and Methodology for River Basin Planning*. Atlanta, Ga.: Water Resources Center, Georgia Institute of Technology, 1964, 561 pp.

Symposium proceedings analyzing primarily the experience in the Southeast River Basins of the United States and the methods used. The discussions include also suggestions toward study format and scope, plan preparation, and practical management of river basins.

71. Klein, L. *River Pollution: Causes and Effects*, Volume II. London: Butterworth, Ltd., 1962, 456 pp. *River Pollution: Control*, Volume III. London: Butterworth, Ltd., 1966, 484 pp.

Books that touch the problem of environmental quality levels repeatedly through discussion of the nature of pollution, its causes, uses of river water, and biological and fishlife requirements; coverage is limited to rivers and the British experience.

*72. Kneese, A. V. *The Economics of Regional Water Quality Management*. Washington, D.C.: Resources for the Future, Inc., The Johns Hopkins Press, 1964, 215 pp.

The work constructs a theoretical structure within which the water pollution control task could be accomplished and discusses the various factors involved, such as off-site costs, private utilization of resources, allocation of the absorption capacity of the environment, user charges, and active public participation. Additional features of the book are the examinations of the Ruhr Valley organization, general pollution problems, and methods of treatment.

73. Knobloch, W. *Handbuch der Gesundheitstechnik*. Berlin: Verlag für Bauwesen, 1963, 480 pp.

A general public health textbook in German that discusses water supply and sewer networks, but concentrates particularly on sanitary facilities inside the house.

74. Koenig, L. *Ultimate Disposal of Advanced Treatment Waste*. Washington, D.C.: PHS Publication 999-WP-3 and 10, 1963 and 1964, 78 and 146 pp.

A comprehensive discussion of the permanent disposal of sludge.

75. Kollar, K. L., and A. F. Volonte. *Regional Construction Requirements for Water and Wastewater Facilities, 1955–1967–1980.*

Washington, D.C.: Business and Defense Services Administration, U.S. Department of Commerce, 1967.

A guide for manufacturers to plan future production of equipment in four Bureau of Census regions. Estimates of construction requirements for collection networks and treatment plants are given.

76. The League of Women Voters. *The Big Water Fight.* Brattleboro, Vt.: The Stephen Greene Press, 1966, 246 pp.

The study records the nationwide experience of the L. of W.V. through one of its annual study projects. The book is a synthesis of the findings of separate local groups; its major strength is a number of documented investigations.

77. Lee, D. B. "A Pollution Control Agency's Public Information Program." *Journal WPCF,* Vol. 35, No. 9 (September 1963), pp. 1133–35.

A report on the work in Florida.

*78. Logan, G. A., et al. (edits.). *Proceedings of the First Conference on Environmental Engineering & Metropolitan Planning.* Evanston, Ill.: Northwestern University Press, 1962, 265 pp.

An attempt to cover the entire pollution control field, including public health, metropolitan organization, water supply, various types of wastes and their disposal, governmental considerations, and similar subjects. Most of the individual presentations succeed in relating the technical and administrative aspects to planning work. While the separate papers do not form a complete entity, this book is practically the only publication that addresses itself to the problems important to the planner in the pollution control field.

79. Loucks, D. P. *Wastewater Treatment Systems Analysis.* Conference Preprint No. 368 (ASCE Water Resources Engineering Conference, Denver, Colorado), May 1966, 35 pp.

A highly mathematical model to predict the probability of having less than any specified dissolved oxygen concentration downstream from a pollution source.

80. Lynn, W. R. "Stage Development of Wastewater Treatment Works." *Journal WPCF,* Vol. 36, No. 6 (June 1964), pp. 722–51.

A discussion that applies systems analysis concepts and statistical models to a programmed improvement sequence.

81. Maas, A. A., et al. *Design of Water-Resource Systems: New Techniques for Relating Economic Objectives, Engineering Analysis and Governmental Planning.* Cambridge, Mass.: Harvard University Press, 1962, 620 pp.

A major and pioneering publication that primarily defines a methodology and develops techniques relating technological, economic, and governmental capabilities and objectives, utilizing conventional methods and simulation models, within a systems framework. Its purpose was to analyze only flood control, irrigation, and power problems.

*82. Marks, R. H. "Waste Water Treatment," A special report in *Power* magazine (June 1967), 32 p.

A well-illustrated, concise description of biochemical processes and treatment methods and equipment; precise definitions of terms.

83. Martin, R. C., et al. *River Basin Administration and the Delaware.* Syracuse, N.Y.: Syracuse University Press, 1960, 390 pp.

A theoretical study of water resource management systems and applications to the Delaware River Basin problems; emphasis is placed on administration and financial considerations.

84. McGauhey, P. H. "Reclamation of Water from Domestic and Industrial Wastes" in *Waste Treatment,* by P. Isaac. New York: Pergamon Press, pp. 429–42.

A general description of water recycling methods and limiting factors; particularly irrigation reuse.

85. Merrell, J. C., Jr., and A. Katko. "Reclaimed Wastewater for Santee Recreational Lakes." *Journal WPCF,* Vol. 38, No. 8 (August 1966), pp. 1310–18.

A discussion and evaluation of the water reuse procedures at Santee.

*86. Metcalf & Eddy. "Sewerage and Sewage Disposal," in *American Civil Engineering Practice,* by R. W. Abbett. New York: John Wiley, 1956, Section 19, Volume II.

The forty-one closely packed pages of this, the most widely used handbook of its type in the United States, describe concisely all aspects of sanitary engineering: from quantities of flow to industrial waste treatment. The compact format does not allow any discussion of peripheral pollution considerations nor does it devote much space to an analysis of implications—it is all straightforward engineering information. The currently available edition is becoming somewhat dated and does not include the more recent developments in treatment processes and in the general approach toward pollution control. Yet, since sanitary engineering techniques do not change that rapidly, it is still the basic reference.

87. Ministry of Housing and Local Government. *Operation and Management of Small Sewage Works.* London: Her Majesty's Stationery Office, 1965, 70 pp.

A technical manual offering a careful step-by-step description of procedures in Britain.

*88. National Association of Counties Research Foundation. *Community Action Program for Water Pollution Control.* Washington, D.C.: 1966, 182 pp.

A reasonably successful attempt to place between two covers all the information and arguments that would be required by a local community leader to enter the arena of liquid waste control. The technical aspects are handled quite briefly in layman's terms, but the chapters (or action guides) on legislation, regional considerations, organization, financial aspects, public education, and staffing are thorough and realistic.

89. Organization for European Economic Co-operation. *Water Supply and Sewage Disposal.* Paris: Technical Assistance Mission No. 46, 1953, 145 pp.

An evaluation of United States practices by a group of European experts who provide comparisons between the experiences of the two areas.

90. "Package Plants for Sewage Treatment." *Public Works,* Vol. 92, No. 4 (April 1961), pp. 111–13.

An inventory of thirteen different units on the market, with descriptions.

91. Parkhurst, J. D., and W. E. Garrison. "Water Reclamation at Whittier Narrows." *Journal WPCF,* Vol. 35, No. 9 (September 1963), pp. 1094–1104.

A discussion of the experience and future plans for water reuse in California.

92. Phelps, E. B., *Public Health Engineering.* New York: John Wiley, 1948, 655 pp.

A general discussion of environmental subjects covering all the standard topics; it is particularly strong on biochemical information with respect to sewage characteristics and treatment processes.

93. Pipes, W. O. *Waste-Recovery Processes for a Closed Ecological System.* Washington, D.C.: National Academy of Sciences, National Research Council, Bulletin No. 898, 1961, 22 pp.

A complete description of a proposed recycling system of liquid, solid, and gaseous wastes for a spacecraft.

94. "Pollution: Everybody's Adversary." Special Report of *Today's Health* (March 1966), pp. 38–65.

A series of articles on air, land, water, and food pollution; considerations of water reuse.

95. Pöpel, F. "Sammlung, Aufbereitung und Verwertung fester und flüssiger Siedlungsabfälle," in *Medizin und Städtebau.* München: Verlag von Urban & Schwarzenberg, 1957, pp. 355–404.

A concise, overall view of waste collection and disposal, in German, as a chapter in a monumental book devoted to urban sanitation.

96. Rich, L. G., et al. *Waste Disposal on Space Craft and Its Bearing on Terrestrial Problems.* Washington, D.C.: U.S. Dept. of HEW, Public Health Service, August 1965, 14 pp.

An outline of regenerative systems for all wastes in a closed environment.

97. Rickles, R. N. *Pollution Control.* Pearl River, N.J.: Noyes Development Corp., 1965, Chemical Process Monograph No. 10, 207 pp.

A useful reference consolidating technical information from primary sources in an outline format relying primarily on tables and illustrations.

98. Rudolfs, W. *Industrial Wastes: Their Disposal and Treatment.* Valley Stream, N.Y.: Library of Engineering Classics, 1961, 497 pp.

A general technical source on industrial liquid waste problems; descriptions of processes for specific types of wastes.

*99. Salvato, J. A., Jr. *Environmental Sanitation.* New York: John Wiley, 1958, 660 pp.

A comprehensive investigation of individual water supply and sewage disposal systems, privies, food protection, swimming pools, refuse disposal, and similar health topics; plus considerations of facility locations and healthful housing design incorporating the appropriate sanitary improvements. It is probably the most widely used public health reference in the country.

100. Salvato, J. A., Jr. "Problems of Wastewater Disposal in Suburbia." *Public Works,* Vol. 95, No. 3 (March 1964), pp. 120–21, 172–78.

The case for municipal sewer planning and construction in fringe areas; caveats with respect to septic tanks and suggested procedures under specific conditions.

101. Sebastian, S., and I. C. Buchanan. "Feasibility of Concrete Septic Privies for Sewage Disposal in Anguilla, B.W.I." *Public Health Reports,* Vol. 80, No. 12 (December 1965), pp. 1113–18.

An evaluation of a controlled experiment in a hot climatic zone.

102. Seelye, E. E. "Drainage and Sewerage," in *Design.* New York: John Wiley, 1960, Section 18.

This widely used engineering reference offers definitions, outline descriptions, tables, graphs, and drawings without any discussion. Thus it provides precise design data for specific problems. Section 18 contains information on the collection networks and their elements.

103. Seelye, E. E. "Sewage Treatment," in *Design*. New York: John Wiley, 1960, Section 19.

Same as above. Section 19 covers the various methods and pieces of equipment used for sewage purification, laboratory procedures, and sewage and industrial waste characteristics.

104. Select Committee on National Water Resources, U.S. Senate. *Present and Prospective Means for Improved Reuse of Water*. Washington, D.C.: March 1960, Water Resources Activities in the U.S., Bulletin No. 30, 54 pp.

A basic source providing a broad survey of the reuse problem, methods, and potentialities.

105. *Sewerage Manual and Catalog File*. Ridgewood, N.J.: Public Works Journal Corp., 1965, 282 pp.

The reference lists and describes all pieces of equipment and supplies currently on the market and provides also brief discussions of various processes, methods, and sanitary concepts.

106. Shapiro, J., and R. Ribeiro. "Algal Growth and Sewage Effluent in Potomac Estuary." *Journal WPCF*, Vol. 37, No. 7 (July 1965), pp. 1034–43.

The precise results of experimentation with concentrations of phosphorus.

107. Shuval, H. I. "Water Pollution Control in Semi-Arid and Arid Zones," in *Water Research*. New York: Pergamon Press, 1967, Volume 1, pp. 297–308.

A thorough analysis of the experience in Israel with wastewater irrigation and recharge.

108. Smolensky, J., and F. B. Haar. *Principles of Community Health*. Philadelphia: Saunders, 1967, 515 pp.

A standard text discussing all public health aspects, including environmental sanitation, with descriptions of organizational and administrative structures.

109. Stander, G. J., and P. G. J. Meiring. "Employing Oxidation Ponds for Low Cost Sanitation." *Journal WPCF*, Vol. 37, No. 7 (July 1965), pp. 1025–33.

A discussion of simple sewage disposal methods in hot climatic zones.

110. State of New York, Dept. of Health. *Sewage Disposal Systems for the Home*. Albany, n.d., Part III, Bulletin No. 1, 27 pp.

A brief manual for septic tank design.

111. State of New York, Dept. of Health. *Standards for Waste Treatment Works,* Albany, 1965, Bulletin 1 in 3 parts, 65, 14, and 23 pp.

The official New York State standards, procedures, and plan formats for major waste treatment works as well as individual household systems.

112. Stead, F. M. "Levels of Environmental Health." *American Journal of Public Health,* Vol. 50, No. 3 (March 1960), pp. 312–15.

An article constructing a framework for analysis that is a lucid approach toward structuring the task of pollution control by defining levels of concern and suggesting corresponding programs.

113. Steel, E. W. *Water Supply and Sewerage.* New York: McGraw-Hill, 1968, 655 pp.

One of the standard sanitary engineering texts used in colleges, handling both aspects of water use in one volume.

114. Stein, M. "Legislation on Water Pollution Control." *Public Health Reports,* Vol. 79, No. 8 (August 1964), pp. 699–706.

A review of Federal legislation and suggested state control acts, enforcement procedures, and aid for public works.

115. Stewart, G. R. *Not So Rich As You Think.* Boston, Mass.: Houghton Mifflin Co., 1968, 248 pp.

Another well-written example of the "literature of protest," attempting not only to sketch the dimensions of the problem but also to explain our negligence and complacency.

116. Still, H. *The Dirty Animal.* New York: Hawthorn Books, Inc., 1967, 298 pp.

A well-documented survey of land, air, and water pollution and the automobile problem for the popular market; an evaluation of current programs.

117. Subcommittee on Municipal Sewer Ordinances, WPCF. *Regulation of Sewer Use.* Washington, D.C.: WPCF, 1963, Manual of Practice No. 3, 41 pp.

A complete proposed ordinance on sewers that supplies explanations of each clause allowing a municipality to regulate the construction and the use of sewer systems by individual property owners.

118. Subcommittee on Operation of Sewage Plants, WPCF. *Operation of Waste Treatment Plants.* Washington, D.C.: WPCF, 1961, Manual of Practice No. 11, 178 pp.

A detailed technical manual that gives an insight into the actual routine work involved and the complications that may arise.

119. Subcommittee on Science, Research, and Development. *Environ-*

mental Pollution: A Challenge to Science and Technology. Washington, D.C.: Committee on Science and Astronautics, U.S. House of Representatives, 1966, 60 pp.

A summary report on the Congressional hearings investigating the role of technology in pollution control; with recommendations.

120. Subcommittee on Waste Disposal. *Report on Individual Household Aerobic Sewage Treatment Systems*. Washington, D.C.: National Academy of Sciences, National Research Council, 1958, Publication No. 586, 18 pp.

A comprehensive and technical reference on package plants, the processes used and their effectiveness.

121. The Task Force on Environmental Health and Related Problems. *A Strategy for a Livable Environment: A Report to the Secretary of Health, Education and Welfare*. Washington, D.C.: U.S. Dept. of Health, Education and Welfare, June 1967, 90 pp.

A very broad and fundamental evaluation of the effects of the environment on man and vice versa. Suggested goals and strategies.

122. Taylor, F. B. "Governmental Aspects of Sanitation in the Urban Fringe." *Public Health Reports,* Vol. 75, No. 2 (February 1960), pp. 95–102.

The article outlines the various ways, with brief evaluations, through which sanitary sewers may be extended in suburban areas, ranging from annexation to mutual cooperation.

123. Teletzke, G. H. "Packaged Sewage Disposal Plants." *Progressive Architecture* (July 1960), pp. 164–68.

A comprehensive evaluation of package plants.

124. Terry, L. L. "The City in National Health." *Public Health Reports,* Vol. 77, No. 5 (May 1962), pp. 377–82.

An evaluation of metropolitanism as an effect on public health and of the aid programs used in large urbanized areas.

125. Texas Water and Sewage Works Association. *Manual for Sewage Plant Operators*. Austin: Texas State Dept. of Health, 1964, 782 pp.

A technical operational and maintenance manual that includes chapters ranging from public health considerations to the training of personnel.

126. Ullrich, A. H. "Use of Wastewater Stabilization Ponds in Two Different Systems." *Journal WPCF,* Vol. 39, No. 6 (July 1967), pp. 965–77.

A detailed description of the operational and maintenance procedures used in Austin, Texas.

127. U.S. Department of Agriculture. *Water: The Yearbook of Agriculture.* Washington, D.C.: 1955, 751 pp.

A general work that includes a chapter on individual sewage disposal systems together with brief articles on general pollution problems related to farming.

128. U.S. Department of Interior. *Conservation Yearbook,* in four volumes. Washington, D.C.: 1965, 1966, 1966, and 1968; 96, 80, 128, and 100 pp.

Quest for Quality, The Population Challenge, The Third Wave, and *Man. . . . an Endangered Species?*—provide convincing and well-illustrated source material on the dangers facing the natural environment.

129. U.S. Department of the Interior. *New Water for Old.* Washington, D.C.: 1966, 8 pp.

A description of the Lebanon, Ohio, experimental tertiary plant.

130. U.S. Department of Labor. *Labor and Material Requirements for Sewer Works Construction.* Washington, D.C.: 1966, Publication No. 1490, 31 pp.

Statistics on the ratio between labor and material costs in sewerage improvements; also total expenditures in the United States.

131. U.S. Public Health Service. *Environmental Health Planning Guide.* Washington, D.C.: 1962, Publication No. 823, 60 pp.

Despite its title, the work is only a manual on how to prepare sanitation studies on air pollution, housing, refuse, public water supply, and sewerage. It consists primarily of suggested survey forms and illustrative examples.

132. U.S. Public Health Service. *Environment and Health.* Washington, D.C.: 1951, Publication No. 84, 152 pp.

A general overview of the problem; somewhat dated.

*133. U.S. Public Health Service et al. *Manual of Septic Tank Practice.* Washington, D.C.: 1967, Publication No. 526, 92 pp.

The basic definitive reference for individual waste disposal systems, presenting the information in a clear and organized way and making it directly usable for design and review purposes.

134. U.S. Public Health Service. *Modern Sewage Treatment Plants: How Much Do They Cost?* Washington, D.C.: 1964, Publication No. 1229, 37 pp.

The publication provides estimating guides through correlation graphs relating costs to size. The information is based on the records of 1,504 projects executed under the Federal program.

135. U.S. Public Health Service. *Pollutional Effects of Storm Water and*

Overflows from Combined Sewers. Washington, D.C.: 1964, Publication No. 1246, 39 pp.

A report on several field studies which examines existing and possible solutions together with cost analyses.

136. U.S. Public Health Service. *Problems in Financing Sewage Treatment Facilities.* Washington, D.C.: 1962, Publication No. 886, 16 pp.

A discussion of the orthodox methods of financing sanitary improvements, particularly of municipal bonds.

137. U.S. Public Health Service. *Recommended State Legislation and Regulations.* Washington, D.C.: 1965, Publication No. 1451, 109 pp.

A publication that offers drafts of suggested state enabling and control legislation.

138. U.S. Public Health Service. *Report of the Committee on Environmental Health Problems to the Surgeon General.* Washington, D.C.: 1962, 288 pp.

A comprehensive discussion of the various facets of environmental engineering, devoting considerable space to water supply and pollution control.

139. U.S. Public Health Service. *Sewage Treatment Plant Construction Cost Index.* Washington, D.C.: 1963, Publication No. 1069, 33 pp.

Indices which are updated regularly and show the cost trends on an averaged nationwide basis with some breakdown by component parts.

140. U.S. Public Health Service. *Sewer Construction Cost Index.* Washington, D.C.: 1964, Publication No. 1132, 29 pp.

Same as above.

141. U.S. Public Health Service. *Symposium on Environmental Measurements.* Washington, D.C.: 1964, Environmental Health Series.

A brief description and evaluation of methods to measure pollution levels.

142. "Utilities for Subdivisions," in *Home Builders Manual for Land Development.* Washington, D.C.: National Association of Home Builders, 1958, pp. 60–92.

The work includes suggestions for the provision of various utility services in subdivisions; however, the discussion is rather brief and oriented toward minimum costs.

143. Veatch, J. O., and C. R. Humphrys. *Water and Water Use Terminology.* Kaukauna, Wisc.: Thomas Printing and Publishing Co., 1966, 381 pp.

A dictionary of terms with an emphasis on lakes.

144. Wagner, E. G., and J. N. Lanoix. *Excreta Disposal for Rural Areas.* Geneva: 1958, WHO Monograph Series No. 39, 187 pp.

A discussion of basic considerations and descriptions of privies and waterborne systems, organizational aspects, and programs.

*145. *Waste Management: Generation and Disposal of Solid, Liquid and Gaseous Wastes in the New York Region.* Prepared for the Regional Plan Association by B. T. Bower, G. P. Larson, A. Michaels, and W. M. Phillips. A Report of the Second Regional Plan, March 1968, 107 pp.

A pioneering and landmark effort to structure a regional waste control system; an extensive discussion of theory and a plea for more precise data.

146. Water Pollution Control Federation. *Public Relations for Water Pollution Control.* Washington, D.C.: 1961, Publication No. 12, 72 pp.

Suggestions for handling public education campaigns.

147. *Water Resources Thesaurus.* Washington, D.C.: U.S. Dept. of the Interior, Office of Water Resources Research, November 1966, 237 pp.

A compilation of cross-indiced descriptors and terms useful for literature retrieval.

148. Weibel, S. R., et al. "Urban Land Runoff as a Factor in Stream Pollution." *Journal WPCF,* Vol. 36, No. 7 (July 1964), pp. 914–24.

A report on actual study results.

149. Wenten, H. *Kanalisations Handbuch.* Köln: R. Müller, 1965, 205 pp.

A comprehensive sewerage handbook in German that covers all standard topics with great thoroughness, including pipe networks and elements, European construction practices, and treatment facilities.

150. Weston, R. F., et al. "Water Quality Management—Legal, Technical, and Administrative Aspects." *Journal WPCF,* Vol. 36, No. 9 (September 1964), pp. 1082–1106.

The article, while keeping the discussion at a policy level, outlines elements of water rights, use of resources, goals and approaches to overall planning and organization for administration.

151. Wilson, D. R. "Public Relations During Sewer Construction." *Journal WPCF,* Vol. 35, No. 6 (June 1963), pp. 758–61.

A discussion of public information work.

152. Wolman, A. "The Metabolism of Cities." *Scientific American,* Vol. 213, No. 3 (September 1965), pp. 179–90.

A discussion of air and water problems closely related to planning work and studies of urbanism; with examples.

153. World Health Organization. *Environmental Change and Resulting Impacts on Health.* Geneva: 1964, Technical Report Series No. 292, 23 pp.

A brief report of an Expert Committee discussing the general pollution problems.

154. World Health Organization. *Environmental Sanitation.* Geneva: 1950, Technical Report Series No. 10, 33 pp.

A report by an Expert Committee outlining principles and objectives; suggestions for WHO work.

155. World Health Organization. *Environmental Sanitation.* Geneva: 1954, Technical Report Series No. 77, 25 pp.

Same as above.

156. World Health Organization. *Design and Operation of Septic Tanks.* Geneva: 1953, Monograph Series No. 18, 122 pp.

A seminar evaluation of septic tanks that looks at the problem from various sides, including an examination of systems servicing groups of houses.

157. World Health Organization. *Local Health Service.* Geneva: 1960, Technical Report Series No. 194, 49 pp.

A report on a proposed survey of public health aspects including suggestions for administrative organizations and results of pilot studies.

158. World Health Organization. *Medicine and Public Health in the Arctic and Antarctic.* Geneva: 1963, Public Health Paper No. 18, 169 pp.

A conference discussion of sanitation problems in the very cold regions and of medical programs, including sanitary engineering.

159. World Health Organization. *Planning of Public Health Services.* Geneva: 1961, Technical Report Series No. 215, 48 pp.

An evaluation of needed health and sanitary services, proposals toward the establishment of programs, and case studies of actual work.

160. World Health Organization. *Urban Health Services.* Geneva: 1963, Technical Report Series No. 250, 35 pp.

The fifth report in a series on public health administration, stressing organization and financing of health services, including sewerage.

161. World Health Organization. *Water Pollution Control.* Geneva: 1966, Technical Report Series No. 318, 32 pp.

A report by an Expert Committee giving a general survey of the problem and touching upon most of the aspects included in this monograph on a global scale.

INDEX